THE DOWNFALL
OF
ROBERT,
EARLE OF HUNTINGTON

by

ANTHONY MUNDAY

List of Characters

in the order of their appearance

Sir John Eltham
Skelton
Little Tracy   *Characters of the*
Sir Thomas Mantle   *Induction.*
Clown
The other Players, the
characters of the dumbshow
Gilbert de Hood, Prior of York and uncle to Robert, Earl of Huntingdon.
Justice Warman, Steward to Robert, Earl of Huntingdon;
      later Sheriff of Notingham.
Robert Hood, Robert, Earle of Huntingdon.
Little John, his Servant.
Marian, his betrothed
      (after line 781, Matilda, daughter of Lord Fitzwater).
Eleanor, the Queen Mother.
Lord Sentloe
Sir Hugh Lacy   *Conspirators against the*
Sir Gilbert Broghton   *Earl of Huntingdon.*
Mistress Warman.
Prince John.
The Bishop of Ely.
Much, the Miller's Son, a clown.
A messenger from Ely.
Simon, Earl of Leicester
      (after line 781, Lord Salisbury).
Lord Lacy, brother of Sir Hugh and father of Marian
      (after line 781, Lord Fitzwater).
A boy, servant to Sir Hugh Lacy.
Lord Chester.
Friar Tuck.
Ralph, Warman's man.
Scarlet.
Scathlock.

i

First Collier.
Second Collier.
Widow Scarlet, mother of Scarlet and Scathlock.
Sir Doncaster of Hothersfield.
Jinny, daughter of the Widow Scarlet.
A servant of the Prior.
Another servant, messenger from York.
A Herald.
Earl of Leicester.
Richmond.
Warman's Cousin.
Jailer of Notingham.
Mistress Thomson.
King Richard.
Sheriff's men, Sir Doncaster's ruffians, Leicester's drum and ancient, soldiers, officers, attendants, Jailer's dog.

Contents

Scene i

[*Enter Sir John Eltam, and knocke at Skeltons doore.*

Eltham   Howe, maister Skelton? What, at studie hard?

[*Opens the doore.*

 5   **Skelton**   Welcome and wisht for, honest Sir John Eltham
    I have sent twice, and either time
    He mist that went to seeke you.

Eltham   So full well hee might.
    These two howers it pleas'd his Majesty
10   To use my service in survaying mappes
    Sent over from the good King Ferdinand,
    That to the Indies, at Sebastians sute,
    Hath lately sent a Spanish Colonie.

Skelton   Then twill trouble you, after your great affairs,
15   To take the paine that I intended to intreat you to
    About rehearsall of your promis'd play.

Eltham   Nay master Skelton, for the King himselfe,
    As wee were parting, bid mee take great heede
    Wee faile not of our day; therefore I pray

1

20   Sende for the rest that now we may rehearse.

Skelton   O they are readie all, and drest to play.
        What part play you?

Eltham   Why I play Little John
        And came on purpose with this greene sute.

25   **Skelton**   Holla my masters, Little John is come.

        [At every doore all the Players runne out, some
        crying"where? where?" Others welcome Sir John;
        among others the boyes and Clowne.

    Skelton   Faith little Tracy you are somewhat forward:
30   What, our Maid Marian leaping like a lad?
        If you remember, Robin is your love:
        Sir Thomas Mantle yonder, not Sir John.

    Clown   But master, Sir John is my fellowe, for I am
        Much, the Millers sonne. Am I not?

35   **Skelton**   I know yee are, sir,
        And gentlemen, since you are thus prepar'd,
        Goe in and bring your dumbe scene on the stage,
        And I, as Prologue, purpose to expresse
        The ground whereon our historie is laied.

40   *[Exeunt; manet Skelton.*

        [Trumpets sounde; enter first king Richard, with drum
        and Auncient, giving Ely a purse and scepter, his mother,
        and brother John, Chester, Lester, Lacie, others at the
        kings appointment doing reverence. The king goes in;
45   *presently Ely ascends the chaire; Chester, John, and the*
        Queene part displeasantly. Enter Robert, Earle of Hun-
        tington, leading Marian; followes him Warman, and, after
        Warman, the Prior, Warman ever flattering and making
        curtsie, taking gifts of the Prior behinde, and his master
50   *before. Prince John enters, and offereth to take Marian.*

Scene i

Queene Elinor enters, offering to pull Robin from her,
but they infolde each other and sit downe within the
curteines; Warman with the Prior, Sir Hugh Lacy, Lord
Sentloe, & Sir Gilbert Broghton folde hands, and drawing
55 *the curteins, all but the Prior enter and are kindely re-*
ceived by Robin Hoode. The curteins are againe shut.

Skelton Sir John, once more, bid your dumbe shewes come in,
That as they passe I may explane them all.

[Enter King Richard with drumme and scepter, and Ensigne,
60 *giving Ely a purse; his mother and brother John,*
Chester, Lester, Lacie, others at the Kings appointment,
doing reverence. The King goes in.

Richard calde Cor de Lyon takes his leave,
Like the Lords Champion, gainst the Pagan foes
65 That spoyle Judea and rich Palestine.
The rule of England and his princely seate
He leaves with Ely, then Lord Chancellor,
To whom the mother Queene, her sonne, Prince John,
Chester, and all the Peeres are sworne.

70 *[Exit Richard cum militibus.*

[Ely ascends the chaire; Chester, John and the Queene
part displeasantly

Now reverend Ely, like the deputie
Of Gods greate deputie, ascends the throne,
75 Which the Queene mother, and ambitious John
Repining at, rais'd many mutinies;
And how they ended you anone shall heare.

[Exeunt omnes.

[Enter Robert, Earle of Huntington, leading Marian; fol-
80 *lowes him Warman, and after Warman the Prior, War-*
man ever flattering and making curtsie, taking gifts
of the Prior behinde, and his master before. Prince

3

John enters, offereth to take Marian. Queene Elinor
enters, offering to pull Robin from her; but they in-
85   *folde each other, and sit downe within the curteines.*

This youth that leads yon virgin by the hand
(As doth the Sunne, the morning richly clad)
Is our Earle Robert, or your Robin Hoode,
That in those daies was Earle of Huntington.
90   The ill fac't miser, brib'd in either hand,
Is Warman, once the Steward of his house,
Who Judas-like betraies his liberall Lord
Into the hands of that relentlesse Prior,
Calde Gilbert Hoode, uncle to Huntington.
95   Those two that seeke to part these lovely friends
Are Elenor the Queene and John the Prince;
She loves Earle Robert, he Maide Marian,
But vainely: for their deare affect is such,
As only death can sunder their true loves.
100   Long had they lov'd, and now it is agreed
This day they must be troth-plight, after wed.
At Huntingtons faire house a feast is helde,
But envie turnes it to a house of teares.
For those false guestes, conspiring with the Prior,
105   To whome Earle Robert greatly is in debt,
Meane at the banquet to betray the Earle,
Unto a heavie writ of outlawry.
The manner and escape you all shall see.

Eltham   Which all, good Skelton?

110   **Skelton**   Why, all these lookers on,
Whom, if wee please, the King will sure be pleas'd.
Looke to your entrance, get you in Sir John. [*Exit Sir John.*
My shift is long, for I play Frier Tucke,
Wherein if Skelton have but any lucke
115   Heele thanke his hearers oft, with many a ducke.
For many talk of Robin Hood that never shot in his bowe,
But Skelton writes of Robin Hood what he doth truly knowe.
Therefore, I pray yee,
Contentedly stay yee

4

120   And take no offending,
        But sit to the ending.
        Likewise I desire,
        Yea would not admire,
        My rime so I shift.
125   For this is my drift,
        So mought I well thrive,
        To make yee all blithe:
        But if ye once frowne,
        Poore Skelton goes downe,
130   His labour and cost,
        He thinketh all lost,
        In tumbling of bookes
        Of Mary goe lookes.
        The Sheriffe with staves,
135   With catchpoles and knaves,
        Are comming, I see,
        High time tis for mee
        To leave off my babble
        And fond ribble rabble.
140   Therefore with this curtsie
           A while I will leave yee. [*Exit.*

Scene ii

[Enter, as it were in haste, the Prior of Yorke, the
Sheriffe, Justice Warman, steward to Robin Hoode.

Prior   Here master Warman, there's a hundred crowns,
145   For your good will and furtherance in this.

Warman   I thanke you my Lord Prior, I must away
        To shunne suspicion, but be resolute,
        And wee will take him, have no doubt of it.

Prior   But is Lord Sentloe and the other come?

150   **Warman**   Lord Sentloe, Sir Hugh Lacie, and Sir Gilbert Broghton
        Are there and, as they promist you last night,
        Will helpe to take him, when the Sheriffe comes.
           [Exit Warman.

Prior   A while farewell, and thankes to them and you.
        Come master Sheriffe, the outlawry is proclam'd;
155   Sende therefore quickly for more companie,
        And at the backe gate wee will enter in.

Sheriff   Wee shall have much adoe I am afraide.

Prior   No, they are very merry at a feast,
        A feast, where Marian, daughter to Lord Lacy,
160   Is troth-plighted to wastfull Huntington.
        And at the feast are my especiall friends,

Whom hee suspectes not: come weele have him, man,
And for your paines, here is a hundred markes. *Exeunt.*

Sheriff   I thanke your Lordshippe, weele be diligent.

Scene iii

165   *[Enter Robin Hoode, Little John following him -- the one*
Earle of Huntington, the other his servant, Robin having
his napkin on his shoulder, as if hee were sodainly
raised from dinner.

Robin   As I am outlawed from my fame and state,
170   Be this day outlawed from the name of daies:
Day lucklesse, outlawe lawlesse, both accurst.

[Flings away his napkin, hat, and sitteth downe.

Lit. John Doe not forget your honourable state,
Nor the true noblesse of your worthy house.

175   **Robin**   Doe not perswade mee; vaine as vanitie
Are all thy comforts -- I am comfortlesse.

Lit. John Heare mee my Lord.

Robin   What shall I heare thee say?
Alreadie hast thou saide too much to heare.
180   Alreadie hast thou stabd mee with thy tongue,
And the wide wound with words will not be clos'd.
Am I not outlawed, by the Prior of Yorke,

8

Proclaim'd in court, in citie, and in towne,
A lawlesse person? This thy tongue reports:
185 And therefore seeke not to make smooth my griefe:
For the rough storme thy windie words hath rais'd
Will not be calm'd till I in grave be laied.

Lit. John Have patience yet.

Robin   Yea, now indeede thou speakest.
190 Patience hath power to beare a greater crosse
Then honours spoyle, or any earthly losse.

Lit. John Doe so my Lord.

Robin   I, now I would beginne;
But see, another Scene of griefe comes in.

195   [*Enter Marian.*

Marian   Why is my Lord so sad? Wherefore so soone,
So sodainely arose yee from the boorde?
Alas my Robin, what distempering griefe
Drinkes up the roseat colour of thy cheekes?
200 Why art thou silent? Answere mee my love.

Robin   Let him, let him, let him make thee as sad.
Hee hath a tongue can banish thee from joy,
And chase thy crimson colour from thy cheekes.
Why speakest thou not? I pray thee Little John,
205 Let the short story of my long distresse
Be uttered in a word. What mean'st thou to protract?
Wilt thou not speake? Then Marian list to mee.
This day thou wert a maide, and now a spowse,
Anone (poore soule) a widdowe thou must bee:
210 Thy Robin is an outlawe, Marian,
His goods and landes must be extended on,
Himselfe exilde from thee, thou kept from him,

[*She sinkes in his armes.*

9

By the long distance of unnumbred miles.
215   Faint'st thou at this? Speake to mee Marian,
My olde love newely met, parte not so soone;
Wee have a little time to tarry yet.

Marian   If but a little time, let mee not stay,
Part wee today, then will I dye today.

220   **Lit. John**   For shame my Lord, with courage of a man,
Bridle this over-greeving passion,
Or else dissemble it, to comfort her.

Robin   I like thy counsell. Marian, cleare these clouds,
And with the sunny beames of thy bright eyes,
225   Drinke up these mistes of sorrowe that arise.

Marian   How can I joy, when thou art banished?

Robin   I tell thee love, my griefe is counterfaite,
And I abruptly from the table rose,
The banquet being almost at an ende,
230   Onely to drive confused and sad thoughts
Into the mindes of the invited guestes.
For, gentle love, at greate or nuptiall feastes,
With Comicke sportes, or Tragicke stately plaies,
Wee use to recreate the feasted guestes,
235   Which I am sure our kinsfolke doe expect.

Marian   Of this what then? This seemes of no effect.

Robin   Why thus of this, as Little John can tell,
I had bespoken quaint Comedians:
But greate John, John the Prince, my lieges brother,
240   My rivall, Marian, he that crost our love,
Hath crost mee in this jest, and at the court,
Imployes the Players, should have made us sport;
This was the tydings brought by Little John,
That first disturbd mee and begot this thought
245   Of sodaine rysing, which by this I know
Hath with amazement, troubled all our guestes:

Scene iii

Goe in, good love; thou as the Chorus shalt
Expresse the meaning of my silent griefe,
Which is no more but this: I only meane
250   (The more to honour our right noble friends)
Myselfe in person to present some Sceanes
Of tragick matter, or perchance of mirth,
Even such as first shall jumpe with my conceipt.

Marian   May I be bolde thou hast the worst exprest?

255   **Lit. John** Faire mistresse, all is true my Lord hath said.

Robin   It is, it is.

Marian   Speake not so hollow then;
So sigh and sadly speake true sorrowing men.

Robin   Beleeve mee love, beleeve mee (I beseech)
260   My first Scene tragick is, therefore tragicke speech,
And accents, fitting wofull action, I strive to get.
I pray thee sweete goe in, and with thy sight,
Appease the many doubts that may arise.
That done, be thou their usher, bring them to this place,
265   And thou shalt see mee with a loftie verse,
Bewitch the hearers eares and tempt their eyes
To gaze upon the action that I use.

Marian   If it be but a play, Ile play my part:
But sure some earnest griefe affrights my heart.

270   **Lit. John** Let mee intreate yee, Madam, not to feare,
For by the honestie of Little John,
Its but a tragicke Scene we have in hand,
Only to fit the humour of the Queene,
Who is the chiefest at your troth-plight feast.

275   **Marian**   Then will I fetch her Highnesse and the rest.
[Exit Marian.

11

Robin   I, that same jealous Queene, whose doting age
    Envies the choyce of my faire Marian,
    She hath a hande in this.

Lit.John Well, what of that?
280   Now must your honour leave these mourning tunes,
    And thus by my areede you shall provide;
    Your plate and jewels Ile straight packe up,
    And toward Notingham convey them hence,
    At Rowford, Sowtham, Wortley, Hothersfield.
285   Of all your cattell, mony shall be made,
    And I at Mansfield will attend your comming,
    Where weele determine, which waie's best to take.

Robin   Well be it so, a Gods name let it be;
    And if I can, Marian shall come with mee.

290 **Lit.John** Else care will kill her; therefore if you please,
    At th'utmost corner of the garden wall,
    Soone in the evening waite for Marian,
    And as I goe Ile tell her of the place,
    Your horses at the Bell shall readie bee,
295   I meane Belsavage, whence as citizens
    That meant to ride for pleasure some small way,
    You shall set foorth.

Robin   Be it as thou dost say.
    Farewell a while.
300   In spight of griefe, thy love compels mee smile,
    But now our audience comes, wee must looke sad.

    [*Enter Queene Elinor, Marian, Sentloe, Lacie, Brogh-*
    ton, Warman, Robins stewarde. As they meete, John
305   *whispers with Marian.*

    [*Exit John.*

Queene   How now my Lord of Huntington?
    The mistresse of your love, faire Marian,
    Tels us your sodaine rising from the banquet

Was but a humor, which you meane to purge,
310   In some high Tragicke lines, or Comick jests.

Robin   Sit down faire Queen (the Prologues part is plaid,
Marian hath tolde yee, what I bad her tell);
Sit downe Lord Sentloe, cosin Lacy sit,
Sir Gilbert Broghton, yea, and Warman sit;
315   Though you my steward be, yet for your gathering wit,
I give you place, sit downe, sit downe I say,

[*Sets them all downe.*

Gods pittie sit; it must, it must be so:
For you will sit, when I shall stande I knowe.
320   And, Marian, you may sit among the rest,
I pray yee doe, or else rise, stand apart;
These helps shall be beholders of my smart.
You that with ruthlesse eyes my sorrowes see,
And came prepar'd to feast at my sad fall,
325   Whose envie, greedinesse, and jealousie
Afforde mee sorrowe endlesse, comfort small,
Knowe what you knewe before, what you ordaind
To crosse the spousall banquet of my love,
That I am outlawed by the Prior of Yorke,
330   My traiterous uncle, and your trothlesse friend.
Smile you Queene Elinor? laugh'st thou Lord Sentloe?
Lacy look'st thou so blithe at my lament?
Broghton a smooth browe graceth your sterne face:
And you are merry Warman at my mone.
335   The Queene except, I doe you all defie.
You are a sort of fawning sycophants,
That while the sunshine of my greatnesse dur'd,
Reveld out all my day for your delights,
And now yee see the blacke night of my woe
340   Oreshade the beautie of my smiling good,
You to my griefe adde griefe, and are agreed
With that false Prior, to reprive my joyes
From execution of all happinesse.

Warman   Your honour thinks not ill of mee, I hope.

13

345 **Robin** Judas speakes first, with "Master, is it I?"
    No, my false Steward, your accounts are true.
    You have dishonoured mee, I worshipt you.
    You from a paltry pen and inkhorne clarke,
    Bearing a buckram satchell at your belt,
350   Unto a Justice place I did preferre,
    Where you unjustly have my tenants rackt,
    Wasted my treasure and increast your store.
    Your sire contented with a cottage poore,
    Your mastershippe hath halles and mansions built,
355   Yet are you innocent, as cleare from guilt,
    As is the ravenous mastife that hath spilt
    The bloode of a whole flocke, yet slily comes
    And couches in his kennell with smeard chaps
    Out of my house, for yet my house it is,
360   And followe him yee catchpole bribed groomes;
    For neither are ye Lords, nor Gentlemen,
    That will be hired to wrong a Nobleman.
    For hir'd yee were last night, I knowe it I,
    To be my guests, my faithlesse guestes this day,
365   That your kinde hoste you trothlesse might betray:
    But hence, and helpe the Sheriffe at the doore,
    Your worst attempt; fell traitors, as you bee,
    Avoide, or I will execute yee all,
    Ere any execution come at mee, [*Runne away.*
370   They ran away, so ends the tragedie.
    Marian, by Little John, my minde you know,
    If you will, doe: if not, why, be it so. [*Offers to goe in.*

   Queene No words to me Earle Robert ere you goe?

   Robin O to your Highnesse? Yes, adieu proud Queene;
375   Had not you bene, thus poore I had not beene. [*Exit.*

   Queene Thou wrongst mee Robert, Earle of Huntington,
    And were it not for pittie of this maide,
    I would revenge the words that thou hast saied.

   Marian Adde not, faire Queene, distresse unto distresse;

380   But if you can, for pittie make his lesse.

Queene   I can and will forget deserving hate,
        And give him comfort in this wofull state.
        Marian, I knowe Earle Roberts whole desire
        Is to have thee with him from hence away;
385   And though I loved him dearely to this day,
        Yet since I see hee dearlier loveth thee,
        Thou shalt have all the furtherance I may.
        Tell mee, faire girle, and see thou truly tell,
        Whether this night, tomorrowe, or next day,
390   There be no pointment for to meete thy love.

Marian   There is, this night there is, I will not lie,
        And be it disappointed, I shall die.

Queene   Alas poore soule, my sonne, Prince John my son,
        With severall troupes hath circuited the court,
395   This house, the citie, that thou canst not scape.

Marian   I will away with death, though he be grim,
        If they deny mee to goe hence with him.

Queene   Marian, thou shalt go with him clad in my attire,
        And for a shift, Ile put thy garments on,
400   It is not mee, my sonne John doth desire;
        But Marian it is thee he doteth on.
        When thou and I are come into the field,
        Or any other place where Robin staies,
        Mee in thy clothes, the ambush will beset,
405   Thee in my roabes they dare not once approach:
        So while with mee a reasoning they stay,
        At pleasure thou with him maist ride away.

Marian   I am beholding to your Majesty,
        And of this plot will sende my Robin worde.

410 **Queene**   Nay, never trouble him, least it breede suspect:
        But get thee in, and shift of thy attire,
        My roabe is loose, and it will soone be off,

Goe gentle Marian, I will followe thee,
And from betrayers hands will set thee free.

415   **Marian**   I thanke your Highnesse, [*Aside*] but I will not trust ye,
My Robert shall have knowledge of this shift:
For I conceive alreadie your deepe drift.
          [*Exit.*   *intention;*

    Queene   Now shall I have my will of Huntington,
Who taking mee this night for Marian,
420   Will harry mee away in steade of her:
For hee dares not stand trifling to conferre:
Faith, prettie Marian, I shal meete with you,
And with your lovely sweete heart Robert too:
For when wee come unto a baiting place,
425   If with like love my love hee doe not grace,
Of treason capitall I will accuse him,
For traiterous forcing me out of the court,
And guerdon his disdaine with guiltie death,
That of a Princes love so lightly weighes.
          [*Exit.*

Scene iv

430   *[Enter Little John, fighting with the Sheriffe and his men,*
            Warman perswading him.

    Lit. John   Warman, stand off, tit tattle, tel not me what ye can do:
        The goods I say are mine, and I say true.

    Warman   I say the Sheriffe must see them ere they goe.

435   **Lit. John**   You say so Warman; Little John saies no.

    Sheriff   I say I must for I am the kings Shrieve.

    Lit. John   Your must is false, your office I beleeve.

    Watch   Downe with him, downe with him.

    Lit. John   Ye barke at me like curres, but I will downe
440   With twentie stand-and-who-goe-theres of you,
        If yee stand long tempting my patience.
        Why, master Shrive, thinke you mee a foole?
        What justice is there you should search my trunkes,
        Or stay my goods, for that my master owes?

445   **Sheriff**   Here's Justice Warman, steward to your Lord,
        Suspectes some coyne, some jewels, or some plate

17

That longs unto your Lord, are in your trunkes,
And the extent is out for all his goods:
Therefore wee ought to see none be convaid.

450   **Warman**   True, Litle John, I am the sorier.

       Lit. John   A plague upon ye else, how sore ye weepe?
Why, say thou, upstart, that there were some helpe,
Some little little helpe in this distresse,
To aide our Lord and master comfortlesse;
455   Is it thy part, thou screenfac't snotty nose,
To hinder him that gave thee all thou hast?

       [*Enter Justice Warmans wife, odly attyred.*

       Wife   Who's that husband? You, you, means he you?

       Warman   I, ber Lady is it, I thanke him.

460   **Wife**   A, ye kneve you, Gods pittie hisband, why dis not
your worshippe sende the kneve to Newgate?

       Lit.John   Well master Sheriffe, shall I passe or no?

       Sheriff   Not without search.

       Lit.John   Then here the casket stands,
465   Any that dares unto it set their hands,
Let him beginne.

       Wife   Doe hisband, you are a Majestie, y'warrant ther's
olde knacks, cheins, and other toyes.

       Lit.John   But not for you, good Madam beetle browes.

470   **Wife**   Out upon him. By my truly master Justice, and ye
doe not clap him up, I will sue a bill of remorse, and never come betweene a pere of sheetes with yee. Such a
kneve as this, downe with him I pray.

Scene iv

[Set upon him. He knockes some downe.

475   **Wife**   A good Lord, come not neere good hisband, only
charge him; charge him. A good God; helpe, helpe.

*[Enter Prince John, the Bishoppe of Ely, the Prior of
Yorke, with others. All stay.*

Pr. John   What tumult have wee here? Who doth resist
480   The kings writs with such obstinate contempt?

Wife   This knave.

Warman   This rebell.

Pr. John   How now Little John,
Have you no more discretion than you shewe?

485   **Ely**   Lay holde, and clappe the traitor by the heeles.

Lit.John   I am no traitor, my good Lord of Ely,
First heare mee, then commit me if you please.

Pr. John   Speake and be briefe.

Lit.John   Heere is a little boxe,
490   Containing all my gettings twentie yeare;
Which is mine owne, and no mans but mine owne.
This they would rifle, this I doe defend,
And about this we only doe contend.

Pr. John   You doe the fellow wrong: his goods are his;
495   You only must extend upon the Earles.

Prior   That was my Lord; but nowe is Robert Hood,
A simple yeoman as his servants were.

Wife   Backe with that legge, my Lord Prior:
There be some that were his servantes thinke foule
500   scorne to be cald yeomen.

Prior   I cry your worshippe mercy, mistresse Warman.
The squire your husband was his servant once.

Lit.John   A scurvie squire, with reverence of these Lords.

Wife   Doo's he not speake treason, prey.

505   **Ely**   Sirra, yea are too saucie; get you hence.

Warman   But heare mee first, my Lords, with patience.
This scoffing carelesse fellowe, Little John,
Hath loaden hence a horse, twixt him and Much,
A silly rude knave, Much the millers sonne.

510   *[Enter Much, clowne.*

Much   I am here to answere for myselfe, and have taken you in two lies at once. First, Much is no knave,
neither was it a horse Little John and I loded, but a
little curtaile, of some five handfuls high, sib to the Apes
515   onely beast at Parish garden.

Lit.John   But master Warman, you have loded carts
And turnd my Lords goods to your proper use.
Who ever hath the right, you doe the wrong,
And are . . .

520   **Wife**   What is hee kneve?

Lit.John   Unworthy to be named a man.

Much   And Ile be sworne for his wife,

Wife   I, so thou maist Nich.

Much   That shee sets newe markes of all my olde ladies
525   linnen (God rest her soule) and my young Lord never
had them since.

Wife   Out, out, I tooke him them but to whiting, as
God mende mee.

Ely   Leave off this idle talke. Get yee both hence.

530   **Lit.John**   I thanke your honours. Wee are not in love with
being here; wee must seeke service that are master-
lesse.   *[Exeunt Much, John.*

Ely   Lord Prior of Yorke, here's your commission.
You are best make speede, least in his country houses,
535   By his appointment, all his heards be solde.

Prior   I thanke your Honour, taking humble leave. *[Exit.*

Ely   And master Warman, here's your Patent seald,
For the high Sheriffewick of Notingham:
Except the King our master doe repeale
540   This gift of ours.

Pr. John   Let him the while possesse it.

Ely   A Gods name, let him; he hath my good will.   *[Exit.*

Pr. John   Well Warman, this proude Priest I can not brooke.
But to our other matter, send thy wife away.

545   **Warman**   Goe in good wife, the Prince with mee hath
private conference.

Wife   By my troth yee will anger mee: now yee have
the Paterne, yee should call mee nothing but mistresse
Sheriffe: for I tell you I stand upon my replications.

550   *[Exit.*

Pr. John   Thinkest thou that Marian meanes
To scape this evening hence with Robin Hoode?
[Warman]   The horse boy tolde mee so, and here he comes,
Disguised like a citizen me thinkes.

21

555   **[Pr. John]** Warman, lets in. Ile fit him presently;
         Only for Marian am I now his enemie.   [*Exeunt.*

Scene v

[Enter Robin like a citizen.

Robin   Earle John and Warman, two good friends of mine:
          I thinke they knewe mee not, or if they did
560   I care not what can followe. I am sure
          The sharpest ende is death, and that will come.
          But what of death or sorrowe doe I dreame?
          My Marian, my faire life, my beautious love,
          Is comming, to give comfort to my griefe,
565   And the sly Queene, intending to deceive,
          Hath taught us how we should her sleights receive.
                    [Enter John.
          But who is this? Gods pittie, here's Prince John.
          We shall have some good rule with him anone.

Pr. John God even, sir; this cleare evening should portend
570   Some frost I thinke. How judge you honest friend?

Robin   I am not weatherwise; but it may be,
          Wee shall have hard frost. For true charitie,
          Good dealing, faithfull friendshippe, honestie,
          Are chil-colde, deade with colde.

575 **Pr. John** O good sir, stay.
          That frost hath lasted many a bitter day.
          Knowe yee no frozen hearts that are belov'd?

23

Robin   Love is a flame, a fire, that being mov'd,
            Still brighter growes; but say, are you belov'd?

580   **Pr. John** I would be, if I be not; but passe that.
            Are ye a dweller in this citie, pray?

Robin   I am, and for a gentlewoman stay,
            That rides some foure or five mile in great haste.

[*Enter Queene, Marian.*

585   **Pr. John** I see your labour, sir, is not in waste.
            For here come two: are either of these yours?

Robin   Both are, one must.

Pr. John Which doe you most respect?

Robin   The youngest and the fairest I reject.

590   **Pr. John** [*Aside*] Robin, Ile try you whether yee say true.

Robin   [*Aside*] As you with mee, so John Ile jeast with you.

Queene   Marian, let me goe first to Robin Hood,
            And I will tell him what wee doe intend.

Marian   Doe what your Highnesse please. Your will is mine.

595   **Pr. John** My mother is with gentle Marian;
            O it doth grieve her to be left behinde.

Queene   Shall we away my Robin, least the Queene
            Betray our purpose? Sweete, let us away.
            I have great will to goe, no heart to stay.

600   **Robin**   Away with thee? No! Get thee farre away
            From mee foule Marian, faire though thou be nam'd,
            For thy bewitching eyes have raised stormes,
            That have my name and noblesse ever sham'd.

Scene vi

Prince John, my deare friend once, is now, for thee,
605   Become an unrelenting enemie,

Pr. John   But Ile relent, and love thee, if thou leave her.

Robin   And Elinor, my soveraignes mother Queene,
That yet retaines true passion in her breast,
Stands mourning yonder. Hence, I thee detest.
610   I will submit mee to her Majestie.
Greate Princesse, if you will but ride with mee,
A little of my way, I will expresse
My folly past, and humble pardon beg.

Marian   I grant, Earle Robert, and I thanke thee too.

615   **Queene**   She's not the Queene, sweete Robin, it is I.

Robin   Hence sorceresse, thy beauty I defie.
If thou have any love at all to mee,
Bestowe it on Prince John: he loveth thee.

   [Exeunt Robin, Marian.

620   **Pr. John**   And I will love thee Robin, for this deede,
And helpe thee too, in thy distressefull neede.

Queene   Wilt thou not stay nor speake, proud Huntington?
Ay mee, some whirlwinde hurries them away.

Pr. John   Follow him not, faire love, that from thee flies:
625   But flie to him that gladly followes thee.
Wilt thou not, girle? Turnst thou away from mee?

Queene   Nay, we shall have it then,
If my queint sonne, his mother gin to court.

Pr. John   Wilt thou not speake, faire Marian, to Prince John,
630   That loves thee well?

Queene   Good sir, I know you doe.

25

Pr. John   That can maintaine thee?

Queene   I, I know you can:
       But hitherto I have maintained you.

635   **Pr. John**   My princely mother?

Queene   I, my princely sonne.

Pr. John   Is Marian then gone hence with Huntington?

Queene   I, she is gone, ill may they either thrive.

Pr. John   Mother, they must goe whom the divell drives.
640   For your sharpe furie, and infernall rage,
         Your scorne of mee, your spite to Marian,
         Your over-doting love to Huntington,
         Hath crost yourselfe, and mee it hath undone.

Queene   I, in mine owne deceipt, have met deceipt.
645   In briefe, the manner thus I will repeate;
         I knewe, with malice that the Prior of Yorke
         Pursu'd Earle Robert; and I furdred it,
         Though God can tell, for love of Huntington.
         For thus I thought, when he was in extreames,
650   Neede, and my love would winne some good regarde
         From him to mee, if I reliev'd his want.
         To this end came I to the mock-spouse feast;
         To this end made I change for Marians weede,
         That me, for her, Earle Robert should receive.
655   But now I see they both of them agreed,
         In my deceipt, I might myselfe deceive.
         Come in with mee, come in and meditate
         How to turne love, to never changing hate. [*Exit.*

Pr. John   In by yourselfe; I passe not for your spels.
660   Of youth and beautie still you are the foe.
         The curse of Rosamond rests on your head,
         Faire Rose confounded by your cankers hate. *cankerous;*

O that she were not as to mee she is,
A mother, whom by nature I must love,
665 Then would I tell her shee were too too base,
To dote thus on a banisht carelesse groome:
Then should I tell her that shee were too fond,
To thrust faire Marian to an exiles hand.

[*Enter a messenger from Ely.*

670 **Messenger** My Lord, my Lord of Ely sends for you,
About important businesse of the state.

Pr. John Tell the proude prelate I am not dispos'd,
Nor in estate to come at his commaunde.

[*Smite him, hee bleedes.*

675 Be gon with that, or tarry and take this.
Zwouns, are yee listning for an after-arrant?
[*Exit Messenger.*
Ile followe, with revengefull murdrous hate,
The banisht, beggerd, bankrout Huntington.

[*Enter Simon, Earle of Leicester.*

680 **Leicester** How now, Prince John? Bodie of mee, I muse
What mad moodes tosse yee, in this busie time,
To wound the messenger that Ely sent,
By our consents? Yfaith yee did not well.

Pr. John Leyster, I meant it Ely, not his man:
685 His servants heade but bleedes; hee headlesse shall
From all the issues of his traitor necke,
Poure streames of bloode, till he be bloodlesse left.
By earth it shall, by heaven it shall be so,
Leister, it shall though all the world say no.

690 **Leicester** It shall, it shall, but how shall it be done?
Not with a stormie tempest of sharpe words,
But slowe, still speaches, and effecting deedes.

Here comes olde Lacy and his brother Hugh.
One is our friend, the other is not true.

695   [*Enter Lord Lacy, Sir Hugh, and his boy.*

Lacy   Hence trechor as thou art! By Gods blest mother
Ile lop thy legges off, though thou be my brother,
If with thy flatring tongue thou seeke to hide
Thy traiterous purpose. Ah poore Huntington,
700   How in one houre have villaines thee undone?

Hugh   If you will not beleeve what I have sworne,
Conceipt your worst. My Lord of Ely knowes
That what I say is true.

Lacy   Still facest thou?
705   Drawe boy, and quickly see that thou defende thee.

Leicester Patience, Lord Lacy, get you gon, Sir Hugh,
Provoke him not, for he hath tolde you true.
You knowe it, that I knowe the Prior of Yorke,
Together with my good Lord Chauncellor,
710   Corrupted you, Lord Sentloe, Broghton, Warman,
To feast with Robert on his day of fall.

Hugh   They lie that say it; I defie yee all.

Pr. John   Now by the Roode thou lyest. Warman himselfe,
That creeping Judas, joyed, and tolde it mee.

715   **Lacy**   Let mee, my Lords, revenge me of this wretch,
By whome my daughter and her love were lost.

Pr. John   For her, let mee revenge with bitter cost.
Shall Sir Hugh Lacy and his fellowes buy
Faire Marians losse, lost by their treachery.
720   And thus I pay it.

    [*Stabs him. He falles; boy runnes in.*

28

Scene vi

Leicester Sure paiment, John.

Lacy There let the villane lie.
  For this, olde Lacie honours thee, Prince John;
725 One trecherous soule, is sent to answere wrong.

[Enter Ely, Chester, officers, Hugh Lacies boy.

Boy Here, here, my Lord,
  Looke where my master lies.

Ely What murdrous hand hath kild this gentle knight,
730 Good Sir Hugh Lacy, steward of my lands?

Pr. John Ely, he died by this princely hand.

Ely Unprincely deed. Death asketh death you know.
  Arrest him officers.

Pr. John O sir, Ile obey; you will take baile, I hope.

735 **Chester** Tis more, sir, than hee may.

Leicester Chester, he may by lawe, and therefore shall.

Ely Who are his baile?

Leicester I.

Lacy And I.

740 **Ely** You are confederates.

Pr. John Holy Lord, you lye.

Chester Be reverent, Prince John; my Lord of Ely,
  You knowe, is Regent for his Majestie.

Pr. John But here are letters from his Majesty,

29

745   Sent out of Joppa, in the holy land,
      To you, to these, to mee, to all the State,
      Containing a repeale of that large graunt,
      And free authoritie to take the seale,
      Into the hands of three Lords temporall,
750   And the Lord Archbishoppe of Roan, he sent,
      And hee shall yielde it, or as Lacy lies,
      Desertfully, for pride and treason stabd,
      He shall ere long lye. Those that intend as I
      Followe this steely ensigne, lift on high.

755   [*Lifts up his drawne sword:*
           Exit, cum Lester and Lacy.

Ely   A thousand thousand ensignes of sharpe steele,
      And feathered arrowes, from the bowe of death,
      Against proud John, wrongd Ely will imploy.
760   My Lord of Chester, let mee have your aide,
      To lay the pride of haute usurping John.

Chester   Some other course than warre let us bethinke.
      If it may be, let not uncivill broiles,
      Our civill hands defile.

765 **Ely**   God knowes that I,
      For quiet of the realme, would ought forbeare.
      But give mee leave, my noble Lord, to feare,
      When one I dearely lov'd is murdered
      Under the colour of a little wrong
770   Done to the wastfull Earle of Huntington,
      Whom John, I knowe, doth hate unto the death,
      Only for love he beares to Lacies daughter.

Chester   My Lord, its plaine this quarrel is but pickt
      For an inducement to a greater ill;
775   But wee will call the Counsell of Estate,
      At which the mother Queene shall present be.
      Thither by summons shall Prince John be cald,
      Lester, and Lacy, who, it seemes,
      Favour some factious purpose of the Prince.

Scene vi

780   **Ely**   You have advised well, my Lord of Chester;
       And as you counsell, so doe I conclude. [*Exeunt.*

Scene vi

[Enter Robin Hoode, Matilda [i.e., Marian],
at one doore; Little John, and Much the millers
sonne at another doore.

Much   Luck I beseech thee, Marry and amen,
785   Blessing betide hem, it be them indeede,
Ah my good Lord, for and my little Ladie.

Robin   What? Much and John, well met in this ill time.

Lit.John   In this good time my Lord; for being met,
The world shall not depart us till wee die.

790   **Matilda**   Saist thou mee so, John? As I am true maide,
If I live long, well shall thy love be paide.

Much   Well, there be on us, simple though wee stand
here, have as much love in hem as Little John.

Matilda   Much, I confesse thou lovest mee very much,
795   And I will more reward it than with words.

Much   Nay I know that, but wee millers children
love the cogge a little, and the faire speaking.

Robin   And is it possible that Warmans spite
Should stretch so farre, that he doth hunt the lives,
800   Of bonnie Scarlet, and his brother Scathlock.

Much   O, I, sir. Warman came but yesterday to take
charge of the Jaile at Notingham, and this day he saies
he will hang the two outlawes. He meanes to set them
at libertie.

805   **Matilda**   Such libertie God send the pievish wretch
In his most neede.

Robin   Now by my honours hope,
Yet buried in the lowe dust of disgrace,
He is too blame. Say John, where must they die?

810   **Lit.John**   Yonders their mothers house, and here the tree,
Whereon (poore men) they must foregoe their lives.
And yonder comes a lazie, lozell Frier
That is appointed for their confessor,
Who, when we brought your monie to their mothers,
815   Was wishing her to patience for their deaths.

[*Enter Frier Tucke, and Ralphe, Warmans man.*

Ralph   I am timorous, sir, that the prigioners are passed
from the Jaile.

Frier   Soft, sirra, by my order I protest,
820   Ye are too forward; tis no game, no jeast
We goe about.

Robin   Matilda, walke afore,
To widowe Scarlets house. Looke where it stands.
Much, man your Ladie; Little John and I
825   Will come unto you thither presently.

Much   Come Madame, my Lord has pointed the pro-
perer man to goe before yee.

Matilda   Be carefull, Robin, in this time of feare.

[*Exit Much, Matilda.*

830   **Frier**   Now by the reliques of the holy Masse,
A prettie girle, a very bonny lasse.

Robin   Frier, how like you her?

Frier   Mary, by my hoode,
I like her well, and wish her nought but good.

835   **Ralph**   Yee protract, master Frier. I obsecrate ye with
all curtesie, omitting complement, you would vouch,
or deigne to proceede.

Frier   Deigne, vouch, protract, complement, obsecrate?
Why, good man tricks, who taught you thus to prate?
840   Your name, your name, were you never christned?

Ralph   My nomination Radulfe is or Ralph;
Vulgars corruptly use to call mee Rafe.

Frier   O foule corruption of base palliardize,
When idiots witlesse travell to be wise.
845   Age barbarous, times impious, men vitious,
Able to upraise,
Men deade many daies,
That wonted to praise,
The Rimes and the laies
850   Of Poets Laureate,
Whose verse did decorate,
And their lines lustrate
Both Prince and Potentate.
These from their graves,
855   See asses and knaves,
Base idiot slaves,
With boastings and braves,
Offer to upstie,

34

To the heavens hie,
860 With vaine foolery,
And rude ribaldry.
Some of them write
Of beastly delight,
Suffering their lines,
865 To flatter these times,
With Pandarisme base,
And lust doe uncase,
From the placket to the pappe:
God send them ill happe.
870 Some like quaint pedants,
Good wits true recreants,
Yee cannot beseech
From pure Priscian speech.
Divers as nice,
875 Like this odde vice,
Are wordmakers daily.
Others in curtsie
When ever they meete yee,
With newe fashions greete yee,
880 Chaunging each congee,
Sometime beneath knee,
With, good sir, pardon mee,
And much more foolerie,
Paltry, and foppry,
885 Dissembling knavery,
Hands sometime kissing,
But honestie missing.
God give no blessing
To such base counterfaiting.

890 **Lit.John** Stoppe, master Skelton; whither will you runne?

Frier Gods pittie, Sir John Eltam, Little John,
I had forgotte myselfe; but to our play.
Come, good man fashions, let us goe our way,
Unto this hanging businesse. Would, for mee,
895 Some rescue, or repreeve might set them free.

[Exeunt Frier, Ralph.

Robin   Heardst thou not, Little John, the Friers speach,
Wishing for rescue, or a quicke repreeve?

Lit.John   He seemes like a good fellowe, my good Lord.

900   **Robin**   He's a good fellowe, John, upon my word.
Lend mee thy horne, and get thee in to Much,
And when I blowe this horne, come both and helpe mee.

Lit.John   Take heed my Lord: the villane Warman knows you,
And ten to one, he hath a writ against you.

905   **Robin**   Fear not; below the bridge a poore blind man doth dwell,
With him I will change my habit, and disguise,
Only be readie when I call for yee,
For I will save their lives, if it may bee.

Lit.John   I will doe what you would immediatly. *[Exeunt.*

Scene vii

910   *[Enter Warman, Scarlet, and Scathlock bounde, Frier*
            Tuck as their confessor, Officers with halberts.

Warman   Master Frier, be briefe, delay no time.
            Scarlet and Scathlock, never hope for life.
            Here is the place of execution,
915   And you must answere lawe for what is done.

Scarlet   Well, if there be no remedie, we must,
            Though it ill seemeth, Warman, thou shouldst bee
            So bloodie to pursue our lives thus cruellie.

Scathlock Our mother sav'd thee from the gallowes, Warman;
920   His father did preferre thee to thy Lord.   *get advancement for*
            One mother had wee both, and both our fathers,
            To thee and to thy father, were kinde friends.

Frier   Good fellowes, here you see his kindnesse ends.
            What he was once, hee doth not now consider.
925   You must consider of your many sinnes;
            This day, in death, your happinesse beginnes.

Scarlock If you account it happinesse, good Frier,
            To beare us companie, I you desire.
            The more the merrier, wee are honest men.

930 **Warman**   Ye were first outlaws, then ye prooved theeves,
            And now all carelessely yee scoffe at death.

Both of your fathers were good honest men;
Your mother lives, their widowe, in good fame.
But you are scapethrifts, unthrifts, villanes, knaves,
935   And, as yee liv'd by shifts, shall die with shame.

Scathlock Warman, good words, for all your bitter deeds.
Ill speach, to wretched men, is more than needs.

[Enter Raphe, running.

Ralph   Sir, retire yee, for it hath thus succeeded, the car-
940   nifex, or executor, riding on an ill curtall, hath tituba-
ted or stumbled, and is now cripplefied, with broken or
fracted tibiards, and sending you tidings of successe, saith,
yourselfe must be his deputie.

Warman   Ill luck! But, sirra, you shall serve the turne.
945   The cords that binde them, you shall hang them in.

Ralph   How are you, sir, of mee opiniated? Not to possesse
your seneschalship, or sherivaltie, not to be Earle of
Notingham, will Ralph be nominated by the base scan-
dalous vociferation of a hangman.

950   *[Enter Robin Hoode, like an old man.*

Robin   Where is the shrieve, kinde friends? I you beseech,
With his good worshippe, let mee have some speech.

Frier   Here is the Sheriffe, father, this is hee.

Robin   Frier, good alms, and many blessings thank thee.
955   Sir, you are welcome to this troublous sheere.
Of this daies execution did I heare.
Scarlet and Scathlocke murdered my young sonne,
Mee have they robd, and helplessely undoone.
Revenge I would, but I am olde and dry:
960   Wherefore, sweete master, for saint charitie,
Since they are bound, deliver them to mee,
That for my sons blood I reveng'd may bee.

Scene vii

Scarlet   This old man lies, we nere did him such wrong.

Robin   I doe not lie, you wote it too too well;
965   The deede was such, as you may shame to tell.
          But I with all intreats might not prevaile
          With your sterne stubborne mindes, bent all to blood.
          Shall I have such revenge then, master Sheriffe,
          That with my sonnes losse, may suffice myselfe?

970   [*Robin whispers with them.*

Warman   Doe, father, what thou wilt, for they must die.

Frier   I never heard them toucht with bloode till now.

Warman   Notorious villanes, and they made their brags,
          The Earle of Huntington would save their lives;
975   But hee is downe the winde, as all such shall,
          That revell, wast and spende, and take no care.

Robin   My horne once winded, Ile unbinde my belt,
          Whereat the swords and bucklers are fast tied.

Scathlock Thankes to your Honour. Father, we confesse,
980   And, were our armes unbounde, we would upheave
          Our sinfull hands with sorrowing hearts to heaven.

Robin   I will unbinde you, with the Sheriffes leave.

Warman   Doe. Helpe him Ralphe; go to them, master Frier.

Robin   And as yee blew your horns, at my sons death,
985   So will I sound your knell, with my best breath.

          [*Sound his horne.*

          And here's a blade, that hangeth at my belt,
          Shall make ye feele in death, what my sonne felt.

39

990

[Enter Little John, Much, Scarlet, and Scathlock. Fight: the
Frier, making as if he helpt the Sheriffe, knockes downe
his men, crying, "Keepe the kings peace."

Ralph   O they must be hangd, father.

Robin   Thy master and thyselfe supply their roomes.
Warman, approach mee not, tempt not my wrath.

995   For if thou doe, thou diest remedilesse.

Warman   It is the outlawed Earle of Huntington;
Downe with him Frier. Oh, thou dost mistake.
Fly Ralph, wee die else; let us raise the shire.

[Sheriffe runnes away, and his men.

1000   **Frier**   Farewell Earle Robert, as I am true frier,
I had rather be thy clarke, then serve the Prior.
                    [Exit Frier.

Robin   A jolly fellowe, Scarlet, knowest thou him?

Scarlet   Hee is of Yorke, and of Saint Maries Cloister.
There where your greedie uncle is Lord Prior.

1005   **Much**   O murren on ye, have you two scap't hanging?
Harke yee, my Lord, these two fellowes kept at Barns-
dale seaven yeare, to my knowledge, and no man.

Robin   Here is no biding masters. Get yee in;
Take a short blessing at your mothers hands.

1010   Much, beare them companie, make Matilda merry.
John and myselfe will followe presently.
                    [Exeunt Much, Scarlet, Scath.
John, on a sodaine thus I am resolv'd,
To keepe in Sherewodde, till the Kings returne,
And being outlawed, leade an outlawes life.

1015   Seaven yeares these brethren, being yeomens sons,
Lived and scap't the malice of their foes.
How thinkest thou, Little John, of my intent?

Lit.John I like your Honours purpose exceeding well.

Robin Nay, no more honour, I pray thee Little John.
1020 Henceforth I will be called Robin Hoode,
Matilda shall be my Maid Marian.
Come, John, friends all, for now beginnes the game,
And after our deserts, so growe our fame. [*Exeunt*

Sceneviii

[*Enter Prince John and his Lords, with souldiers.*

1025 **Pr. John** Now is this comet shot into the sea,
Or lies like slime, upon the sullen earth.
Come, he is deade, else should we heare of him.

Salsbury I knowe not what to thinke herein, my Lord.

Fitzwater Ely is not the man I tooke him for,
1030   I am afraide wee shall have worse than hee.

Pr. John Why, good Fitzwater, whence doth spring your fear?

Fitzwater Him, for his pride, we justly have supprest;
But prouder climers are about to rise.

Salsbury Name them, Fitzwater; know you any such?

1035 **Pr. John** Fitzwater meanes not any thing, I know;
For if he did, his tongue would tell his heart.

Fitzwater An argument of my free heart, my Lord,
That lets the worlde be witnesse of my thought.
When I was taught, true dealing kept the schoole;
1040   Deeds were sworne partners with protesting words.

We said and did, these say and never meane.
This upstart protestation of no proofe,
This, I beseech you, sir, accept my love;
Commaund mee, use mee, O you are too blame
1045   That doe neglect my everlasting zeale,
My deare, my kinde affect, when God can tell,
A sodaine puffe of winde, a lightning flash,
A bubble on the streame doth longer dure,
Than doth the purpose of their promise bide.
1050   A shame upon this peevish apish age,
These crouching hypocrite dissembling times.
Well, well, God rid the patrones of these crimes,
Out of this land. I have an inward feare,
This ill, well-seeming sinne will be bought deare.

1055   **Salsbury** My Lord Fitzwater is inspir'd I thinke.

Pr. John I, with some divell; let the olde foole dote.

[*Enter Queene Mother, Chester, Sheriffe, Kent*
    souldiers.

Queene From the pursuing of the hatefull Priest,
1060   And bootlesse search of Ely are wee come.

Pr. John And welcome is your sacred Majestie.
And, Chester, welcome too, against your will.

Chester Unwilling men come not without constraint,
But uncompeld comes Chester to this place,
1065   Telling thee, John, that thou art much too blame
To chase hence Ely, Chauncelor to the King,
To set thy footesteppes on the cloath of state,
And seate thy body in thy brothers throne.

Salsbury Who should succeede the brother, but the brother?

1070   **Chester** If one were deade, one should succeede the other.

Queene My sonne is king, my son then ought to raigne.

Fitzwater One sonne is king, the State allows not twaine.

Salsbury The subjects many yeares the king have mist.

Chester But subjects must not chuse what king they list.

1075 **Queene** Richard hath conquered kingdomes in the East.

Fitzwater A signe hee will not loose this in the West.

Salsbury By Salsburies honour, I will follow John.

Chester So Chester will, to shunne commotion.

Queene Why? John shall be but Richards deputie.

1080 **Fitzwater** To that, Fitzwater gladly doth agree.
And looke to't Lady, minde King Richards love:
As you will answer't, doe the King no wrong.

Queene Well said old conscience; you keep still one song.

Pr. John In your contentious humours, noble Lords,
1085 Peeres, and upholders of the English State,
John silent stoode, as one that did awaite
What sentence yee determind for my life.
But since you are agreed that I shall beare
The weightie burthen of this kingdomes state,
1090 Till the returne of Richard, our dread king,
I doe accept the charge, and thanke you all,
That think me worthie of so great a place.

All Wee all confirme you Richards deputie.

Salsbury Now shall I plague proud Chester.

1095 **Queene** Sit you sure, Fitzwater.

Chester For peace, I yield to wrong.

Pr. John   Now olde man, for your daughter.

Fitzwater   To see wrong rule, my eyes run streams of water.

[*A noyse within.*

1100   [*Enter a Collier, crying a monster.*

Collier   A monster, a monster! Bring her out Robin, a
monster, a monster!

Salsbury   Peace gaping fellowe. Knowest thou where thou art?

Collier   Why? I am in Kent, within a mile of Dover.
1105   Sbloud, where I am, peace, and a gaping fellow?
For all your dagger, wert not for your ging,
I would knocke my whipstocke on your addle head.
Come out with the monster, Robin.

Within   I come, I come, help mee she scrats.

1110   **Collier**   Ile gee her the lash; come out yee bearded witch.

[*Bring forth Ely, with a yarde in his hand, and linnen cloath, drest like a woman.*

Ely   Good fellowes let mee goe, there's gold to drinke.
I am a man, though in a womans weedes.
1115   Yonders Prince John, I pray yee let mee goe.

Queene   What rude companions have we yonder Salsbury?

1 Coll.   Shall we take his money?

2 Coll.   No, no; this is the thiefe that robd master
Mighels, and came in like a woman in labour, I war-
1120   rant yee.

Salsbury   Who have yee here, honest colliers?

45

2 Coll.   A monster, a monster! A woman with a bearde,
a man in a petticote! A monster, a monster!

Salsbury   What my good Lord of Ely, is it you?
1125   Ely is taken; here's the Chauncelor.

1 Coll.   Pray God wee be not hangd for this tricke?

Queene   What my good Lord?

Ely   I, I, ambitious Ladie.

Pr. John   Who, my Lord Chauncelour?

1130   **Ely**   I, you proud usurper.

Salsbury   What, is your surplesse turned to a smock?

Ely   Peace, Salibury, thou changing weathercocke.

Chester   Alas, my Lord, I grieve to see this sight.

Ely   Chester, it will be day for this darke night.

1135   **Fitzwater** Ely, thou wert the foe to Huntington:
Robin, thou knewest, was my adopted sonne:
O Ely, thou to him wert too too cruell,
With him fled hence Matilda, my faire jewell.
For their wrong, Ely, and thy hautie pride,
1140   I helpt Earle John; but now I see thee lowe,
At thy distresse, my heart is full of woe.

Queene   Needes must I see Fitzwaters overthrowe.
John, I affect him not; he loves not thee.
Remoove him John, least thou remooved bee.

1145   **Pr. John** Mother, let mee alone. By one and one,
I will not leave one, that envies our good.
My Lord of Salsbury, give these honest colliers,

46

Scene viii

For taking Ely, each a hundred markes.

Salsbury   Come fellowes, goe with mee.

1150   **1 Coll.**   Thanke yee faith; farewell, monster.

> [*Exeunt Salsbury, Colliers.*

Pr. John   Sheriffe of Kent, take Ely to your charge,
From Shreeve to Shreeve, send him to Notingham
Where Warman, by our Patent, is high Shreeve.
1155   There as a traitor, let him be close kept,
And to his triall wee will follow straight.

Ely   A traitor, John?

Pr. John   Doe not expostulate.
You at your trial shal have time to prate.   [*Exeunt cum Ely.*

1160   **Fitzwater**   God for thy pittie, what a time is here?

Pr. John   Right gratious mother, wold yourself and Chester
Would but withdrawe you for a little space,
While I conferre with my good Lord Fitzwater.

Queene   My Lord of Chester, will you walke aside?

1165   **Chester**   Whether your Highnesse please, thither I wil.

> [*Exeunt Chester, Queene.*

Pr. John   Souldiers, attend the person of our mother.   [*Exeunt.*
Noble Fitzwater, now wee are alone,
What oft I have desir'd, I will intreate,
1170   Touching Matilda, fled with Huntington.

Fitzwater   Of her what wold you touch? Touching her flight,
She is fledde hence with Robert, her true knight.

Pr. John   Robert is outlawed, and Matilda free.

Why through his fault should she exiled be?
1175   She is your comfort, all your ages blisse.
Why should your age, so great a comfort misse?
She is all Englands beautie, all her pride.
In forren lands, why should that beautie bide?
Call her againe Fitzwater, call againe
1180   Guiltlesse Matilda, beauties souveraigne.

Fitzwater I graunt, Prince John, Matilda was my joy,
And the faire sunne, that kept old winters frost
From griping deade the marrowe of my bones.
And she is gone, yet where she is, God wote,
1185   Aged Fitzwater truly guesseth not.
But where she is, there is kinde Huntington;
With my faire daughter, is my noble sonne.
If he may never be recald againe,
To call Matilda backe it is in vaine.

1190   **Pr. John** Living with him, she lives in vitious state,
For Huntington is excommunicate.
And till his debts be paid, by Romes decree,
It is agreed, absolv'd he can not be.
And that can never be. So never wife,
1195   But in a loath'd adult'rous beggers life,
Must faire Matilda live? This you may amend
And winne Prince John, your ever during friend.

Fitzwater As how, as how?

Pr. John Cal her from him; bring her to Englands court,
1200   Where, like faire Phoebe, she may sit as Queene,
Over the sacred honourable maids
That doe attend the royall Queene, my mother.
There shall shee live a Princes Cynthia,
And John will be her true Endimion.

1205   **Fitzwater** By this construction, she should be the Moone,
And you would be the man within the Moone.

Pr. John A pleasant exposition, good Fitzwater:

48

Scene viii

But if it fell so out that I fell in,
You of my full joyes should be chiefe partaker.

1210 **Fitzwater** John, I defie thee. By my honours hope,
I will not beare this base indignitie.
Take to thy tooles. Thinkst thou a noble man
Will be a Pandar to his proper childe?
For what intendst thou else? Seeing I knowe,
1215 Earle Clepstowes daughter is thy married wife.
Come, if thou be a right Plantaginet,
Drawe and defende thee. Oh our Ladie helpe
True English Lords, from such a tyrant Lord.
What, doest thou thinke I jeast? Nay by the Roode,
1220 Ile loose my life, or purge thy lustfull bloode.

Pr. John What my olde Ruffian, lye at your warde?
Have at your froward bosome, olde Fitzwater.

[*Fight: John falles. Enter Queene, Chester, Salsbury
hastily.*

1225 **Fitzwater** O that thou werte not Royal Richards brother,
Thou shouldst here die in presence of thy mother.

[*John rises. All compasse Fitzwater; Fitzwater chafes.*

What, is he up? Nay Lords, then give us leave.

Chester What meanes this rage Fitzwater?
1230 **Queene** Lay hands upon the Bedlam, traitrous wretch.

Pr. John Nay, hale him hence, and heare you old Fitzwater;
See that you stay not five daies in the Realme,
For if you doe, you die remedilesse.

Fitzwater Speak Lords. Do you confirme what he hath said?

1235 **All** He is our Prince, and he must be obaid.

Fitzwater Harken, Earle John, but one word will I say.

49

Pr. John   I will not heare thee, neither will I stay.
　　　Thou knowest thy time.　　　　　　　*[Exit.*

Fitzwater   Will not your Highnesse heare?

1240 **Queene**   No, thy Matilda robd mee of my deare. *[Exit.*

Fitzwater   I aided thee in battell, Salsbury.

Salsbury   Prince John is moov'd; I dare not stay with thee.
　　　　　[Exit Salsbury.

Fitzwater   Gainst thee and Ely, Chester, was I foe?
　　　And dost thou stay to aggravate my woe?

1245 **Chester**   No, good Fitzwater, Chester doth lament
　　　Thy wrong, thy sodaine banishment.
　　　Whence grue the quarrell twixt the Prince and thee?

Fitzwater   Chester, the divell tempted old Fitzwater,
　　　To be a Pandar to his only daughter,
1250　　　And my great heart, impatient, forst my hand,
　　　In my true honours right, to chalenge him.
　　　Alas the while, wrong will not be reproov'd.

Chester   Farewell, Fitzwater. Wheresoere thou bee,
　　　By letters, I beseech thee, send to mee.　*[Exit.*

1255 **Fitzwater**   Chester, I will, I will.
　　　Heavens turne to good this woe, this wrong, this ill.
　　　　[Exit.

Scene ix

1260

[Enter Scathlocke and Scarlet, winding their hornes at severall doores. To them enter Robin Hoode, Matilda all in greene, Scathlockes mother, Much, Little John, all the men with bowes and arrowes.

Robin Widowe, I wish thee homeward now to wend,
Least Warmans malice worke thee any wrong.

Widow Master I will, and mickle good attend
On thee, thy love, and all these yeomen strong.

Matilda Forget not, widowe, what you promise mee.

Much O I, mistresse, for Gods sake lets have Jinny.

Widow You shall have Jinny sent you with all speede.
Sonnes farewell, and by your mothers reede,
Love well your master: blessing ever fall
On him, your mistresse, and these yeomen tall.
[*Exit.*   *brave*

Much God be with you, mother; have much minde I
pray on Much, your sonne, and your daughter Jinny.

Robin Wind once more, jolly huntsmen, all your horns,

51

1275   Whose shrill sound, with the ecchoing wods assist,
                  Shall ring a sad knell for the fearefull deere,
                  Before our feathered shafts, deaths winged darts,
                  Bring sodaine summons for their fatall ends.

Scarlet   Its ful seaven years since we were outlawed first,
1280   And wealthy Sherewood was our heritage.
                  For all those yeares we raigned uncontrolde,
                  From Barnsdale shrogs to Notinghams red cliffes;
                  At Blithe and Tickhill were we welcome guests.
                  Good George a Greene at Bradford was our friend,
1285   And wanton Wakefields Pinner lov'd us well.
                  At Barnsley dwels a Potter tough and strong,
                  That never brookt we brethren should have wrong.
                  The Nunnes of Farnsfield, pretty nunnes they bee,
                  Gave napkins, shirts, and bands to him and mee.
1290   Bateman of Kendall, gave us Kendall greene,
                  And Sharpe of Leedes, sharpe arrowes for us made:
                  At Rotheram dwelt our bowyer, God him blisse.
                  Jackson he hight; his bowes did never misse.
                  This for our good, our scathe let Scathlocke tell,
1295   In merry Mansfield, how it once befell.

Scathlock In merry Mansfield, on a wrestling day,
                  Prizes there were, and yeomen came to play.
                  My brother Scarlet and myselfe were twaine.
                  Many resisted, but it was in vaine,
1300   For of them all we wonne the mastery,
                  And the gilt wreathes were given to him and mee.
                  There by Sir Doncaster of Hethersfield,
                  Wee were bewraid, beset, and forst to yield,
                  And so borne bound, from thence to Notingham,
1305   Where we lay doom'd to death, till Warman came.

Robin   Of that enough. What cheere, my dearest love?

Much   O good cheare anone, sir, she shall have venson
her bellyfull.

Matilda   Matilda is as joyfull of thy good,

1310   As joy can make her. How fares Robin Hood?

Robin   Well, my Matilda, and if thou agree,
          Nothing but mirth shall waite on thee and mee.

Marian   O God, how full of perfect mirth were I,
          To see thy griefe turnd to true jollitie!

1315 **Robin**   Give me thy hand; now Gods curse on me light,
          If I forsake not griefe, in griefes despight.
          Much, make a cry, and yeomen stand yee round.
          I charge yee never more let woefull sound
          Be heard among yee; but what ever fall,
1320   Laugh griefe to scorne; and so make sorrowes small.
          Much, make a cry, and loudly, Little John.

Much   O God, O God, helpe, helpe, helpe! I am un-
          doone, I am undoone.

Lit.John Why how now, Much? Peace, peace, you roaring
1325   slave.

Much   My master bid mee cry, and I will cry till hee
          bid me leave. Helpe, helpe, helpe: I, mary, will I.

Robin   Peace, Much; reade on the Articles good John.

Lit.John First, no man must presume to call our master,
1330   By name of Earle, Lord, Baron, Knight, or Squire,
          But simply by the name of Robin Hoode.

Robin   Say, yeomen, to this order will ye yielde?

All   We yield to serve our master Robin Hoode.

Lit.John Next tis agreed (if thereto shee agree)
1335   That faire Matilda henceforth change her name,
          And while it is the chance of Robin Hoode,
          To live in Sherewodde a poore outlawes life,
          She, by Maid Marians name, be only cald.

Matilda   I am contented; reade on, Little John,
1340   Henceforth let me be nam'd Maid Marian.

Lit.John   Thirdly, no yeoman, following Robin Hoode
In Sherewod, shall use widowe, wife, or maid,
But by true labour, lustfull thoughts expell.

Robin   How like yee this?

All   Master, we like it well.

Much   But I cry no to it. What shal I do with Jinny then?

Scarlet   Peace, Much; goe forwarde with the orders, fellowe John.

Lit.John   Fourthly, no passenger with whom ye meete
1350   Shall yee let passe till hee with Robin feast --
Except a Poast, a Carrier, or such folke,
As use with foode to serve the market townes.

All   An order which we gladly will observe.

Lit.John   Fiftly, you never shall the poore man wrong,
1355   Nor spare a priest, a usurer, or a clarke.

Much   Nor a faire wench, meete we her in the darke.

Lit.John   Lastly, you shall defend with all your power,
Maids, widowes, orphants, and distressed men.

All   All these wee vowe to keepe, as we are men.

1360 **Robin**   Then wend ye to the Greenewod merrily,
And let the light roes bootlesse from yee runne.
Marian and I, as soveraigns of your toyles,
Will wait, within our bower, your bent bowes spoiles.

Much   Ile among them master.

Scene ix

1365   [*Exeunt winding their hornes.*

Robin   Marian, thou seest though courtly pleasurs want,
        Yet country sport in Sherewodde is not scant.
        For the soule-ravishing delicious sound
        Of instrumentall musique, we have found
1370   The winged quiristers, with divers notes,
        Sent from their quaint recording prettie throats,
        On every branch that compasseth our bower,
        Without commaund, contenting us each hower.
1375   For Arras hangings, and rich Tapestrie,
        We have sweete natures best imbrothery.
        For thy steele glasse, wherein thou wontst to looke,
        Thy christall eyes, gaze in a christall brooke.
        At court, a flower or two did decke thy head:
        Now with whole garlands is it circled.
1380   For what in wealth we want, we have in flowers,
        And what wee loose in halles, we finde in bowers.

Marian   Marian hath all, sweete Robert, having thee,
        And guesses thee as rich, in having mee.

Robin   I am indeede,
1385   For having thee, what comfort can I neede?

Marian   Goe in, goe in.
        To part such true love, Robin, it were sinne. [*Exeunt.*

55

Scene x

[Enter Prior, Sir Doncaster, Frier Tucke.

Prior   To take his bodie, by the blessed Roode,
1390   Twold doe me more than any other good.

Doncaster O tis an unthrift, still the Churchmens foe,
             An ill end will betide him, that I knowe.
             Twas hee that urg'd the king to sesse the clergie
             When to the holy land he tooke his jorney;
1395   And he it is that rescued those two theeves,
             Scarlet and Scathlocke, that so manie grieves
             To churchmen did. And now they say
             Hee keepes in Sherewod, and himselfe doth play
             The lawlesse rener; heare you, my Lord Prior;
1400   He must be taken, or it will be wrong.

Prior   I, and he shall bee to.

Tuck   I, I; soone sed. But ere he be, many wil lie deade --
             Except it be by sleight.

Doncaster I there, there, Frier.

1405 **Tuck**
             The widowe Scarlets daughter, lovely Jinny,

56

Scene x

Loves and is belov'd of Much the millers sonne.
If I can get the girle to goe with mee,
Disguis'd in habit, like a pedlers mort,
1410 Ile serve this execution, on my life,
And single out a time alone to take
Robin, that often carelesse walkes alone.
Why? Answere not. Remember what I saide.
Yonder I see comes Jinny, that faire maide;
If wee agree, then back me soone with aide.

[*Enter Jinny with a fardle.*

Prior   Tuck, if thou doe it . . .

Doncaster Pray you doe not talke;
As we were strangers, let us carelesse walke.

1420 **Jinny**   Now to the greene wodde wend I, God me speede.

Tuck   Amen, faire maid, and send thee, in thy neede,
Much, that is borne to doe thee much good deeds.

Jinny   Are you there, Frier? Nay, then yfaith we have it.

Tuck   What, wenche? My love?

1425 **Jinny**   I, gee't mee when I crave it.

Tuck   Unaskt I offer, pre thee, sweete girle, take it.

Jinny   Gifts stinke with proffer;
foh, Frier, I forsake it.

Tuck   I will be kinde.

Jinny   Will not your kindnesse kill her?

1430 **Tuck**   With love?

Jinny   You cogge.

Tuck   Tut, girle, I am no miller; heare in your eare.

Doncaster [*Aside*] The Frier courts her.

Prior   Tush, let him alone,
1435   He is our Ladies Chaplaine, but serves Jone.

Doncaster Then, from the Friers fault, perchance, it may be
       The proverbe grew, Jone's taken for my Ladie.

Prior   Peace, good Sir Doncaster, list to the end.

Jinny   But meane yee faith and troth, shall I go weye?

1440 **Tuck**   Upon my faith, I doe intend good faith.

Jinny   And shall I have the pinnes and laces too,
       If I beare a pedlers packe with you?

Tuck   As I am holy Frier, Jinny, thou shalt.

Jinny   Well, there's my hand; see, Frier, you do not halt.

1445 **Tuck**   Goe but before into the miry mead,
       And keepe the path that doth to Farnsfield lead.
       Ile into Suthwell, and buy all the knacks,
       That shall fit both of us for pedlers packes.

Jinny   Who be they two that yonder walke, I prey?

1450 **Tuck**   Jinny, I knowe not; be they what they may,
       I care not for them, pre thee doe not stay,
       But make some speede that we were gone away.

Jinny   Wel Frier, I trust you that we go to Sherewod.

Tuck   I, by my beads, and unto Robin Hoode.

Scene x

1455   **Jinny**   Make speede, good Frier.   [*Exit Jinny.*

       Tuck   Jinny, doe not feare.
              Lord Prior, now you heare
              As much as I; get mee two pedlers packes,
              Points, laces, looking glasses, pinnes and knackes:
1460   And let Sir Doncaster with some wight lads,
              Followe us close; and ere these fortie howers,
              Upon my life, Earle Robert shall be ours.

       Prior   Thou shalt have any thing, my dearest Frier,
              And in amends, Ile make thee my subprior.
1465   Come, good Sir Doncaster, and if wee thrive,
              Weele frolicke with the Nunnes of Leeds belive.

       [*Exeunt.*

Scene xi

[*Enter Fitzwater, like an olde man.*

Fitzwater Well did he write, and mickle did he knowe,
1470　　　That said this worlds felicitie was woe,
　　　　Which greatest states can hardly undergoe.
　　　　Whilom Fitzwater in faire Englands court,
　　　　Possest felicitie and happie state;
　　　　And in his hall blithe fortune kept her sport,
1475　　　Which glee, one howre of woe did ruinate.
　　　　Fitzwater once had castles, townes, and towers,
　　　　Faire gardens, orchards, and delightfull bowers;
　　　　But now nor garden, orchard, towne, nor tower
　　　　Hath poore Fitzwater left within his power.
1480　　　Only wide walkes are left mee in the world,
　　　　Which these stiffe limmes wil hardly let me tread;
　　　　And when I sleepe, heavens glorious canopy
　　　　Mee and my mossie coutch doth over-spreade.
　　　　Of this, injurious John can not bereave mee;
1485　　　The aire and earth he (while I live) must leave mee.
　　　　But from the English aire and earth, poore man,
　　　　His tyranny hath ruthlesse thee exil'd.
　　　　Yet ere I leave it, Ile do what I can,
　　　　To see Matilda, my faire lucklesse childe.

[*Curtaines open; Robin Hoode sleepes on a greene*

60

banke, and Marian strewing flowers on him.

And in good time, see where my comfort stands,
And by her lyes dejected Huntington.
Looke how my flower holds flowers in her hands,
1495   And flings those sweetes upon my sleeping sonne.
Ile close mine eyes as if I wanted sight,
That I may see the end of their delight.

[Goes knocking with his staffe.

Marian   What aged man art thou? Or by what chance,
1500   Cam'st thou thus farre into the wailesse wodde?

Fitzwater Widowe or wife, or maiden if thou be,
Lend mee thy hand: thou seest I cannot see.
Blessing betide thee, little feel'st thou want.

With mee, good childe, foode is both hard and scant.
1505   These smooth even vaines, assure mee he is kinde,
What ere he be, my girle, that thee doth finde.
I poore and olde am reft of all earths good
And desperately am crept into this wodde
To seeke the poore mans patron, Robin Hoode.

1510   **Marian**   And thou art welcome, welcome aged man,
I, ten times welcome to Maid Marian.
Sit downe olde father, sit and call me daughter.
O God, how like he lookes to olde Fitzwater!   *[Runs in.*

1515   **Fitzwater** Is my Matilda cald Maid Marian?
I wonder why her name is changed thus.

[Brings wine, meate.

Marian   Here's wine to cheere thy hart. Drink aged man.
There's venson and a knife, here's manchet fine.
Drinke good old man, I pre you drinke more wine.
1520   My Robin stirres, I must sing him a sleepe.

Robin   Nay, you have wak't me Marian with your talke.
What man is that, is come within our walke?

Marian   An aged man, a silly sightlesse man,
Neere pin'd with hunger: see how fast he eates.

1525 **Robin**   Much good may't doe him. Never is good meat
Ill spent on such a stomacke. Father, proface;
To Robin Hood thou art a welcome man.

Fitzwater I thanke you master. Are you Robin Hood?

Robin   Father, I am.

1530 **Fitzwater** God give your soule much good,
For this good meat Maid Marian hath given mee.
But heare you, master, can you tell mee newes,
Where faire Matilda is, Fitzwaters daughter?

Robin   Why? Here she is, this Marian is shee.

1535 **Fitzwater** Why did she chaunge her name?

Robin   What's that to thee?

Fitzwater Yes, I could weepe for griefe that it is so,
But that my teares are all dryed up with woe.

Robin   Why? Shee is cald Maid Marian, honest friend,
1540 Because she lives a spotlesse maiden life,
And shall, till Robins outlawe life have ende,
That he may lawfully take her to wife;
Which, if King Richard come, will not be long;
For, in his hand is power to right our wrong.

1545 **Fitzwater** If it be thus, I joy in her names change.
So pure love in these times is very strange.

Marian   Robin, I thinke it is my aged father.

Scene xi

Robin Tell mee old man, tell me in curtesie.
Are you no other than you seeme to be?

1550 **Fitzwater** I am a wretched aged man, you see.
If you will doe mee ought for charitie,
Further than this, sweete, doe not question mee.

Robin You shall have your desire, but what be these?

[Enter Frier Tucke, and Jinny, like Pedlers,
1555 *singing.*

What lacke ye? What lacke yee? What ist ye wil buy?
Any points, pins, or laces, any laces, points or pins?
Fine gloves, fine glasses, any buskes, or maskes?
Or any other prettie things?
1560 Come chuse for love, or buy for money.
Any cony cony skins,
For laces, points, or pins? Faire maids, come chuse or buy.
I have prettie poting sticks,
And many other tricks, come chuse for love, or buy
1565 for money.

Robin Pedler, I pre thee set thy packe downe here.
Marian shall buy, if thou be not too deare.

Tuck Jinny, unto thy mistresse shewe thy packe;
Master, for you I have a pretty knacke.
1570 From farre I brought it, please you see the same.

[Enter Sir Doncaster,
and others weaponed.

Frier Sir Doncaster, are not we pedlerlike?

Doncaster Yes, passing fit, and yonder is the bower.
1575 I doubt not wee shall have him in our power.

Frier You and your companie were best stand close.

63

Doncaster What shal the watchword be to bring us forth?

Frier Take it, I pray, though it be much more worth.
When I speake that aloude, be sure I serve
1580 The execution presently on him.

Doncaster Frier, looke too't.

Frier Now Jinny to your song. [*Sings.*

[*Enter Marian, Robin.*

Marian Pedler, what prettie toyes have you to sell?

1585 **Frier** Jinny, unto our mistresse shewe your ware.

Marian Come in, good woman. [*Exit.*

Frier Master, looke here, and God give care,
So mote I thee, to her and mee, if ever wee, Robin to
thee, that art so free, meane treachery.

1590 **Robin** On, Pedler, to thy packe;
If thou love mee, my love thou shalt not lacke.

Frier Master, in briefe, there is a theefe, that seekes
your griefe, God send reliefe, to you in neede; for a foule
deede, if not with speede, you take good heede, there is
1595 decreede.
In yonder brake, there lies a snake, that meanes to
take, out of this wodde, the yeoman good, calde Robin Hoode.

Robin Pedler, I pre thee be more plaine: what brake?
1600 What snake? What trappe? What traine?

Frier Robin, I am a holy Frier, sent by the Prior, who
did mee hire, for to conspire thy endlesse woe, and overthrowe; but thou shalt knowe, I am the man whome
Little John from Notingham desir'd to be a clarke to

1605   thee; for hee to mee saide thou wert free, and I did see,
         thy honestie; from gallowe tree, when thou didst free
         Scathlocke and Scarlet certainely.

Robin   Why then it seemes that thou art Frier Tucke.

Frier   Master, I am.

1610   **Robin**   I pray thee, frier, say
         What treachery is meant to mee this day?

Frier   First winde your horne; then drawe your sworde.

         [*Hee windes his horne.*

         For I have given a friers worde
1615   To take your bodie prisoner
         And yield you to Sir Doncaster,
         The envious Priest of Hothersfield,
         Whose power your bushie wodde doth shielde;
         But I will die, ere you shall yield.

1620   [*Enter Little John, &c:*

         And sith your yeomen doe appeare,
         Ile give the watchword without feare.
         Take it I pray thee, though it be more worth.

         [*Rushe in Doncaster with his crue.*

1625   **Doncaster** Smite down, lay hold on outlawed Huntington.

Lit.John Soft, hot spurd priest, tis not so quickly done.

Doncaster Now out alas, the frier and the maide
         Have, to false theeves, Sir Doncaster betraide.
                        [*Exeunt omnes.*

Scene xii

1630
[*Enter John crowned, Queene Elianor, Chester, Salsbury, Lord Prior. Sit down all. Warman stands.*

Pr. John As Gods Vicegerent, John ascends this throne,
His head impal'd with Englands diademe,
And in his hand the awfull rodde of rule,
Giving the humble, place of excellence,
1635   And to the lowe earth, casting downe the proude.

Queene Such upright rule is in each realme allowed.

Pr. John Chester, you once were Elies open friend,
And yet are doubtfull whether he deserve
A publicke triall for his private wrongs.

1640 **Chester** I still am doubtfull, whether it be fit
To punish private faults with publicke shame
In such a person as Lord Ely is.

Prior Yes honorable Chester, more it fits
To make apparant sinnes of mightie men,
1645   And on their persons sharpely to correct
A little fault, a very small defect,
Than on the poore to practise chastisement.
For if a poore man die, or suffer shame,

66

Only the poore and vile respect the same;
1650 But if the mightie fall, feare then besets
The proud harts of the migtie ones, his mates.
They thinke the world is garnished with nets,
And trappes ordained to intrappe their states.
Which feare, in them, begets a feare of ill,
1655 And makes them good, contrary to their will.

Pr. John Your Lordship hath said right. Lord Salsbury,
Is not your minde as ours, concerning Ely?

Salsbury I judge him worthy of reproofe and shame.

Pr. John Warman, bring forth your prisoner, Ely, the Chancellor,
1660 And with him, bring the seale that he detains.
Warman, why goest thou not?

Warman Be good to mee, my Lord.

Pr. John What hast thou done?

Warman Speake for mee, my Lord Prior.
1665 All my good Lords, intreate his Grace for mee.
Ely, my Lord . . .

Pr. John Why? Where is Ely, Warman?

Warman Fled today, this mistie morning he is fled away.

Pr. John O Judas, whom nor friend nor foe may trust,
1670 Thinkst thou with teares and plaints to answere this?
Doe I not knowe thy heart? Doe I not knowe
That bribes have purchast Ely this escape?
Never make anticke faces, never bende
With fained humblesse, thy still crouching knee;
1675 But with fixt eyes unto thy doome attend.
Villane, Ile plague thee for abusing mee.
Goe hence, and henceforth never set thy foote
In house or fielde, thou didst this day possesse.
Marke what I say; advise thee to looke too't,

67

1680   Or else be sure thou diest remedilesse.
     Nor from those houses see that thou receive
     So much as shall sustaine thee for an hower;
     But as thou art, goe where thou canst get friends,
     And hee that feedes thee, be mine enemie.

1685 **Warman** O, my good Lord.

     Pr. John Thou thy good Lord betrayedst,
     And all the world for money thou wilt sell.

     Warman What saies the Queene?

     Queene Why thus I say:
1690   Betray thy master, thou wilt all betray.

     Warman My Lords, of Chester and of Salsbury?

     Both Speake not to us, all traitors we defie.

     Warman Good my Lord Prior.

     Prior Alas, what can I doe?

1695 **Warman** Then I defie the worlde; yet I desire
     Your Grace would read this supplication.

      [*John reades.*

     Pr. John I thought as much; but Warman dost thou thinke
     There is one moving line to mercie here?
     I tell thee no; therefore away, away.
1700   A shamefull death followes thy longer stay.

     Warman O poore poore man!
     Of miserable, miserablest wretch I am. [*Exit.*

     Pr. John Confusion be thy guide; a baser slave
1705   Earth cannot beare. Plagues followe him, I crave.
     Can any tell mee if my Lord of Yorke

Be able to sit up.

Queene The Archbishoppes Grace
Was reasonable well even now, good sonne.

1710 **Salsbury** And he desir'd mee that I should desire
Your Majestie to send unto his Grace,
If any matter did import his presence.

Pr. John Wee will ourselves steppe in and visit him.
Mother, and my good Lords, will you attend us?

1715 **Prior** I gladly will attend your Majestie.

Pr. John Now good Lord helpe us.
When I saide good Lords,
I meant not you Lord Prior. Lord I know you are;
But good, God knowes, you never meane to bee.

1720 [*Exeunt John, Queene, Chester, Salsbury.*

Prior John is incenst, and very much I doubt
That villane Warman hath accused mee,
About the scape of Ely. Well, suppose he have.
Whats that to mee? I am a cleargie man,
1725 And all his power, if hee all extend,
Cannot prevaile against my holy order;
But the Archbishoppes Grace is now his friend
And may perchance attempt to doe me ill.

[*Enter a serving man.*

1730 What newes with you, sir?

Servant Even heavie news, my Lord; for the light fire
Falling, in manner of a fier drake,
Upon a barne of yours, hath burnt six barnes,
And not a strike of corne reserv'd from dust.
1735 No hand could save it, yet ten thousand hands,
Labourd their best, though none for love of you.

For every tongue with bitter cursing band,
Your Lordshippe as the viper of the land.

Prior   What meant the villanes?

1740   **Servant**   Thus and thus they cride:
Upon this churle, this hoorder up of corne,
This spoyler of the Earle of Huntington,
This lust-defiled, mercilesse false Prior,
Heaven raigneth vengeance downe in shape of fier.
1745   Old wives that scarce could with their crouches creep,   *crutches*
And little babes, that newly learnde to speake,
Men masterlesse that thorough want did weepe,
All in one voice, with a confused cry,
In execrations band you bitterly,
1750   Plague followe plague, they cry, he hath undone
The good Lord Robert, Earle of Huntington,
And then . . .

Prior   What then, thou villane? Get thee from my sight.
They that wish plagues, plagues wil upon them light.

1755   [*Enter another servant.*

What are your tidings?

Servant 2 The Covent of Saint Maries are agreed
And have elected, in your Lordshippes place,
Olde Father Jerome, who is stald Lord Prior,
1760   By the newe Archbishoppe.

Prior   Of Yorke thou meanst.
A vengeance on him, he is my hopes foe.

[*Enter a Herald.*

Herald   Gilbert de Hood, late Prior of Saint Maries,
1765   Our Soveraigne John commandeth thee by mee,
That presently thou leave this blessed land,
Defiled with the burden of thy sinne.

Scene xii

	All thy goods temporall and spirituall,
	With free consent of Hubert Lorde Yorke,
1770	Primate of England and thy Ordinary,
	He hath suspended, and vow'd by heaven,
	To hang thee up, if thou depart not hence,
	Without delaying or more question.
	And that he hath good reason for the same,
1775	He sends this writing firm'd with Warmans hand,
	And comes himselfe, whose presence if thou stay,
	I feare this sunne will see thy dying day.

Prior   O, Warman hath betraid mee. Woe is mee.

[Enter John, Queene, Chester, Salsbury.

1780 **Pr. John**   Hence with that Prior, sirra do not speake,
My eyes are full of wrath, my heart of wreake.
Let Lester come; his hault hart, I am sure,
Will checke the kingly course we undertake.

[Exeunt cum Prior.

1785 *[Enter Lester, drumme and Ancient.*

Pr. John   Welcome from warre, thrice noble Earle of Lester;
Unto our court, welcome, most valiant Earle.

Leicester   Your court in England, and King Richard gone,
A king in England, and the king from home:
1790 This sight and salutations are so strange,
That what I should, I know not how to speake.

Pr. John   What would you say? Speake boldly, we intreat.

Leicester   It is not feare, but wonder barres my speach;
I muse to see a mother and a Queene,
1795 Two peeres, so great as Salsbury and Chester,
Sit and support proud usurpation,
And see King Richards crowne, worne by Earle John.

Queene He sits as viceroy and a substitute.

Chester He must and shal resigne when Richard comes.

1800 **Salsbury** Chester, he will without your must and shall.

Leicester Whether he will or no, he shall resigne.

Pr. John You knowe your own will Lester, but not mine.

Leicester Tell me among ye, where is reverent Ely,
Left by our dreade King, as his deputie?

1805 **Pr. John** Banisht he is, as proud usurpers should.

Leicester Pride then, belike, was enemy to pride:
Ambition in yourselfe, his state envied.
Where is Fitzwater, that old honoured Lord?

Pr. John Dishonourd and exil'd, as Ely is.

1810 **Leicester** Exil'd he may be, but dishonourd never.
He was a fearelesse souldier, and a vertuous scholler.
But where is Huntington, that noble youth?

Chester Undoone by ryot.

Leicester Ah, the greater ruth.

1815 **Pr. John** Lester, you question more than doth become you.
On to the purpose, why you come to us.

Leicester I came to Ely, and to all the State,
Sent by the King, who three times sent before,
To have his ransome brought to Austria;
1820   And if you be elected deputie,
Doe as you ought, and send the ransome money.

Pr. John Lester, you see I am no deputie;
And Richards ransome if you doe require,

Thus wee make answere: Richard is a king,
1825   In Cyprus, Acon, Acres, and rich Palestine.
To get those kingdomes England lent him men,
And many a million of her substance spent,
The very entrals of her wombe was rent.
No plough but paid a share, no needy hand,
1830   But from his poore estate of penurie,
Unto his voyage offered more than mites,
And more, poore soules, than they had might to spare.
Yet were they joyfull. For still flying newes,
And lying I perceive them now to be,
1835   Came of King Richards glorious victories,
His conquest of the Souldans, and such tales
As blewe them up with hope, when he returnd
He would have scattered gold about the streetes.

Leicester Doe Princes fight for gold? O leaden thought!
1840   Your father knewe that honour was the aime
Kings levell at. By sweete Saint John I sweare,
You urge mee so that I cannot forbeare.
What doe you tell of money lent the King,
When first he went into this holy warre?
1845   As if he had extorted from the poore,
When you, the Queene, and all that heare me speake,
Know with what zeale the people gave their goods:
Olde wives tooke silver buckles from their belts,
Young maids the gilt pins that tuckt up their traines,
1850   Children their prettie whistles from their neckes,
And every man what he did most esteeme,
Crying to souldiours, "Weare these gifts of ours."
This prooves that Richard had no neede to wrong
Or force the people that with willing hearts
1855   Gave more than was desir'd. And where you say,
You guesse Richards victories but lies,
I sweare he wan rich Cyprus with his sworde.
And thence, more glorious than the guide of Greece
That brought so huge a fleete to Tenedos,
1860   He saild along the Mediterran sea,
Where on a sunbright morning he did meete
The warlike souldiours well prepared fleete.

O still mee thinkes I see King Richard stand,
In his guilt armour staind with Pagans blood,
1865   Upon a gallies prowe, like warres fierce god,
And on his crest, a crucifix of golde.
O that daies honour can be never tolde:
Six times six severall brigandines he boarded,
And in the greedie waves flung wounded Turkes,
1870   And three times thrice the winged gallies bankes,
(Wherin the Souldans sonne was Admirall)
In his owne person royall Richard smooth'd,
And left no heathen hand to be upheav'd
Against the Christian souldiers.

1875   **Pr. John** Lester, so,
Did he all this?

Leicester I, by God hee did,
And more than this; nay jeast not at it, John:
I sweare hee did, by Lesters faith hee did,
1880   And made the greene sea red with Pagan blood,
Leading to Joppa glorious victory,
And following feare that fled unto the foe.

Pr. John All this hee did, perchance all this was so.

Leicester Holy God helpe mee, souldiers come away:
1885   This carpet knight sits carping at our scarres,
And jeasts at those most glorious well fought warres.

Pr. John Lester, you are too hot. Stay, goe not yet.
Me thinkes, if Richard wonne these victories,
The wealthie kingdomes he hath conquered
1890   May better than poore England pay his ransome.
He left this realme as a young orphant maid
To Ely, the stepfather of this state,
That stript the virgin to her very skinne.
And, Lester, had not John more carefull bin
1895   Than Richard, at this hower, England had not England bin.
Therefore, good warlike Lord, take this in briefe:
We wish King Richard well,

Scene xii

But can send no reliefe.

Leicester O, let not my heart breake with inward griefe.

1900   **Pr. John** Yes let it, Lester, it is not amisse
That twenty such hearts breake, as your heart is.

Leicester Are you a mother? Were you Englands Queene?
Were Henry, Richard, Gefferey (your sonnes)
All sonnes, but Richard, sunne of all those sonnes?
1905   And can you let this little meteor,
This *ignis fatuus*, this same wandring fire,
This goblin of the night, this brand, this sparke,
Seeme through a lanthorne, greater than he is?
By heaven you doe not well, by earth you doe not.
1910   Chester, nor you, nor you, Earle Salsbury,
Ye doe not, no yee doe not what yee should.

Queene Were this Beare loose, how he wold tear our mawes!

Chester Pale death and vengeance dwel within his jawes.

Salsbury But we can muzzle him and binde his pawes;
1915   If King John say we shall, wee will indeede.

Pr. John Doe if you can.

Leicester Its well thou hast some feare.
No curres, ye have no teethe to baite this Beare.
I will not bid mine ensigne bearer wave
1920   My tottered colours in this worthlesse aire
Which your vile breathes vilely contaminate.
Beare, thou hast bene my auncient bearer long,
And borne up Lesters Beare in forren lands.
Yet now resigne these colours to my hands.
1925   For I am full of griefe and full of rage.
John, looke upon mee: thus did Richard take
The coward Austrias colours in his hand,
And thus he cast them under Acon walles,
And thus he trod them underneath his feete.

1930   Rich colours, how I wrong ye by this wrong!
         But I will right yee. Beare, take them againe,
         And keepe them ever, ever them maintaine.
         We shall have use for them I hope, ere long.

     Pr. John   Darest thou attempt thus proudly in our sight?

1935   **Leicester**   What ist a subject dares, that I dare not?

     Salsbury   Dare subjects dare, their soveraigne being by?

     Leicester   O God, that my true soveraigne were ny.

     Queene   Lester, he is.

     Leicester   Madam, by God you ly.

1940   **Chester**   Unmannerd man.

     Leicester   A plague of reverence,
         Where no regard is had of excellence.   [*Sound drum.*
         But you will quit mee nowe; I heare your drummes,
         Your principalitie hath stird up men.
1945   And now ye thinke to muzzle up this Beare.
         Still they come nearer, but are not the neare.

     Pr. John   What drums are these?

     Salsbury   I thinke some friends of yours
         Prepare a power to resist this wrong.

1950   **Leicester**   Let them prepare; for Lester is preparde,
         And thus he wooes his willing men to fight;
         Souldiers, yee see King Richards open wrong,
         Richard that led yee to the glorious East,
         And made yee treade upon the blessed land,
1955   Where He, that brought all Christians blessednesse,
         Was borne, lived, wrought His miracles, and died,
         From death arose, and then to heaven ascended;
         Whose true religious faith ye have defended.

76

Yee fought, and Richard taught yee how to fight
1960　Against prophane men following Mahomet.
But if ye note, they did their kings their right,
These more than heathen, sacrilegious men,
Professing Christ, banish Christs champion hence,
Their lawfull Lord, their homeborne soveraigne,
1965　With pettie quarrels, and with slight pretence.

[*Enter Richmond, souldiers.*

O let me be as short as time is short,
For the arm'd foe is now within our sight.
Remember how gainst ten, one man did fight,
1970　So hundreds against thousands, have borne head.
You are the men that ever conquered.
If multitudes oppresse ye that ye die,
Lets sell our lives and leave them valiantly.
Courage; upon them, till wee cannot stand.

1975　**Pr. John**　Richmond is yonder.

Queene　I, and sonne, I thinke,
The King is not farre off.

Chester　Now heaven forfend.

Leicester　Why smite ye not, but stand thus cowardly?

1980　**Richmond**　If Richmond hurt good Lester, let him die.

Leicester　Richmond, O pardon mine offending eye,
That tooke thee for a foe; welcome deare friend;
Where is my Soveraigne Richard? Thou and he
Were both in Austria. Richmond, comfort mee,
1985　And tell mee where he is, and how he fares.
O, for his ransome, many thousand cares
Have mee afflicted.

Richmond　Lester, he is come to London,
And will himselfe to faithlesse Austria,

1990   Like a true king, his promis'd ransome beare.

Leicester At London saist thou, Richmond, is he there?
Farewell, I will not stay to tell my wrongs,
To these pale coloured, hartlesse, guiltie Lords.
Richmond, you shall goe with mee, doe not stay,
1995   And I will tell you wonders by the way.

Richmond The King did doubt you had some injury,
And therefore sent this power to rescue yee.

Leicester I thanke his Grace. Madam adieu, adieu.
Ile to your sonne, and leave your shade with you.

2000   [*Exeunt.*

Pr. John Harke how he mocks mee, calling me your shade.
Chester and Salsbury, shall wee gather power,
And keepe what we have got?

Chester And in an hower,
2005   Be taken, judg'd, and headed with disgrace?
Salsbury, what say you?

Salsbury My Lord, I bid your excellence adieu --
I to King Richard will submit my knee,
I have good hope his Grace will pardon mee.

2010 **Chester** And Salsbury, Ile goe along with thee.
Farewell, Queene mother; fare you well, Lord John.
     [*Exeunt.*

Pr. John Mother, stay you.

Queene Not I sonne, by Saint Anne.

Pr. John Will you not stay?

2015 **Queene** Goe with me. I will doe the best I may,
To beg my sonnes forgivenesse of my sonne. [*Exit.*

Scene xii

Pr. John Goe by yourselfe. By heaven twas long of you,
          I rose to fall so soone. Lester and Richmonds crue,
          They come to take me. Now too late I rue
2020   My proud attempt. Like falling Phaeton,
          I perish from my guiding of the sunne.
                [Enter Lester and Richmond.

Leicester I will goe backe yfaith once more and see,
          Whether this mock-king and the mother Queene,
          And, who! Heres neither Queene nor Lord.
2025   What, king of crickets, is there none but you?
          Come off, off. This crowne, this scepter are King Richards right.
          Beare thou them, Richmond, thou art his true knight.
          You would not send his ransome, gentle John.
          He's come to fetch it now. Come, wily Fox,
2030   Now you are stript out of the Lyons case,
          What, dare you looke the Lyon in the face?
          The English Lyon, that in Austria,
          With his strong hand, puld out a lyons heart.
          Good Richmond tell it mee; for Gods sake doe:
2035   Oh, it does mee good to heare his glories tolde.

Richmond Lester, I saw King Richard with his fist,
          Strike deade the sonne of Austrian Leopold,
          And then I sawe him, by the Dukes commaund,
          Compast and taken by a troope of men,
2040   Who led King Richard to a lyons denne,
          Opening the doore and in a paved court,
          The cowards left King Richard weaponlesse.
          Anone comes forthe the fier-eyde dreadfull beast,
          And with a heart-amazing voice he roarde,
2045   Opening (like hell) his iron-toothed jawes,
          And stretching out his fierce death-threatning pawes,
          I tell thee Lester, and I smile thereat,
          (Though then, God knowes, I had no power to smile)
          I stoode by treacherous Austria all the while.
2050   Who in a gallery with iron grates,
          Staid to beholde King Richard made a prey.

Leicester What wast, thou smilest at in Austria?

Richmond   Lester, he shooke, so helpe me God, he shooke,
With very terrour, at the Lyons looke.

2055 **Leicester** Ah coward; but goe on what Richard did.

Richmond   Richard about his right hand wound a scarfe
(God quit her for it) given him by a maide,
With endlesse good may that good deede be paid,
And thrust that arme downe the devowring throat
2060 Of the fierce Lyon, and withdrawing it,
Drewe out the strong heart of the monstrous beast,
And left the senselesse bodie on the ground.

Leicester O royall Richard! Richmond, looke on John.
Does he not quake in hearing this discourse?
2065 Come, we will leave him; Richmond, let us goe.
John, make sute for grace, that is your means you knowe.

   [*Exeunt.*

Pr. John A mischiefe on that Lester. Is he gone?
I were best goe too, lest in some mad fit
2070 He turne againe and leade me prisoner.
Southward I dare not flie; faine, faine I would
To Scotland bend my course; but all the woddes
Are full of outlawes that in Kendall greene
Followe the outlawed Earle of Huntington.
2075 Well, I will cloath myselfe in such a sute,
And by that meanes as well scape all pursuite,
As passe the daunger-threatning Huntington.
For having many outlawes theyl thinke mee,
By my attire, one of their mates to be.   [*Exit.*

Scene xiii

2080   [*Enter Scarlet, John, and Frier Tucke*.

Frier   Scarlet and John, so God me save,
              No minde unto my beades I have.
              I thinke it be a lucklesse day,
              For I can neither sing, nor say,
2085   Nor have I any power to looke,
              On Portasse, or on Mattins booke.

Scarlet   What is the reason, tell us Frier?

Frier   And would yee have mee be no lyer.

Lit.John No: God defend that you should lie,
2090   A Churchman be a lyer? Fie.

Frier   Then by this hallowed Crucifixe,
              The holy water, and the pixe,
              It greatly at my stomacke stickes,
              That all this day we had no guesse,
2095   And have of meate so many a messe.

              [*Much brings out Ely, like a country man with*

81

a basket.

Much   Well, and ye be but a market, ye are but a market
man.

2100   **Ely**   I am sure, sir; I doe you no hurt, doe I?

Scarlet   Wee shall have company, no doubt.
My fellowe Much hath founde one out.

Frier   A fox, a fox! As I am Frier,
Much is well worthie of good hire.

2105   **Lit.John**   Say, Frier, soothly knowest thou him?

Frier   It is a wolfe in a sheepes skinne.
Goe call our master, Little John,
A glad man will he be anone.
It's Ely man, the Chancelor.

2110   **Lit.John**   Gods pittie looke unto him, Frier.   [*Exit John.*

Much   What, ha ye egges to sell, old fellowe?

Ely   I, sir, some fewe, and those my neede constraines
mee beare to Mansfield,
That I may sell them there, to buy me bread.

2115   **Scarlet**   Alas good man: I pre the, where dost dwell?

Ely   I dwell at Oxen sir.

Scarlet   I knowe the towne.

Much   Alas poore fellow, if thou dwell with Oxen,
It's strange they doe not gore thee with their hornes.

2120   **Ely**   Masters, I tell yee truly where I dwell,
And whether I am going; let mee goe:
Your master would be much displeas'd I knowe,

Scene xiii

If he should heare, you hinder poore men thus.

Frier   Father, one word with you before we part.

2125   **Much**   Scarlet, the Frier will make us have anger all.
    Farewell, and beare me witnesse, though I staid him,
    I staid him not.
    An olde fellowe, and a market man?   [*Exit.*

Frier   Whoop! In your riddles, Much? Then we shall ha't.

2130   **Scarlet**   What dost thou Frier? Pre thee, let him goe.

Frier   I pre the, Scarlet, let us two alone.

Ely   Frier, I see thou knowest me; let me goe,
    And many a good turne I to thee will owe.

Frier   My masters service bids me answere no;
2135   Yet love of holy churchmen wils it so.
    Well, good my Lord, I will doe what I may
    To let your holinesse escape away.

    [*Enter Robin and Little John.*

    Here comes my master, if he question you,
2140   Answere him like a plaine man, and you may passe.

Ely   Thankes, Frier.

Frier [*Aside*] O, my Lord thinkes me an Asse.

Robin   Frier, what honest man is there with thee?

Frier   A silly man, good master. I will speake for you.
2145   [*Aside*] Stand you aloofe, for feare they note your face.
    Master in plaine, it were but in vaine, long to detaine,
    with toyes and with bables, with fond fained fables: but
    him that you see, in so mean degree, is the Lord Ely, that
    helpt to exile you, that oft did revile you. Though in his

2150   fall, his traine be but small, and no man at all, will give
       him the wall, nor Lord doth him call. Yet he did ride,
       on Jennets pide, and knightes by his side, did foote it
       each tide: O see the fall of pride.

       Robin Frier, enough.

2155 **Frier** I pray, sir, let him goe.
       He is a very simple man in showe;
       He dwelles at Oxen and to us doth say
       To Mansfield market he doth take his way.

       Lit.John Frier, this is not Mansfields market day.

2160 **Robin** What would hee sell?

       Frier Egges sir, as he saies.

       Robin Scarlet, goe thy waies, take in this olde man,
       Fill his skinne with venson:
       And after give him money for his egges.

2165 **Ely** No, sir, I thanke you. I have promised them
       To master Bailies wife of Mansfield, all.

       Robin Nay, sir, you doe me wrong.
       No Baily, nor his wife, shall have an egge.
       Scarlet, I say, take his egges and give him money.

2170 **Ely** Pray, sir.

       Frier Tush, let him have your egges.

       Ely Faith, I have none.

       Frier Gods pittie, then he will finde you soone.

       Scarlet Here are no egges, nor any thing but hay.
2175   Yes, by the masse, here's somewhat like a seale.

Robin   O God, my Princes seale, faire Englands royall seale!
Tell mee, thou man of death, thou wicked man,
How cam'st thou by this seale? Wilt thou not speake?
Bring burning irons, I will make him speake.
2180   For I doe knowe the poore distressed Lord,
The Kings Vicegerent, learned reverend Ely,
Flying the furie of ambitious John,
Is murdred by this peasant. Speake vile man,
Where thou hast done thrice honorable Ely?

2185   **Ely**   Why dost thou grace Ely with stiles of Grace,
Who thee with all his power sought to disgrace?

Robin   Belike his wisdome sawe some fault in mee.

Ely   No I assure thee honorable Earle:
It was his envie, no defect of thine,
2190   And the perswasions of the Prior of Yorke,
Which Ely now repents; see, Huntington,
Ely himselfe, and pittie him, good sonne.

Robin   Alas for woe, alack that so greate state
The malice of this world should ruinate.
2195   Come in, great Lord, sit downe and take thy ease,
Receive the seale and pardon my offence.
With me you shall be safe and if you please,
Till Richard come, from all mens violence.
Aged Fitzwater, banished by John,
2200   And his faire daughter shall con verse with you;
I and my men that me attend upon
Shall give you all that is to honour due.
Will you accept my service, noble Lord?

Ely   Thy kindnesse drives me to such inward shame,
2205   That for my life I no reply can frame.
Goe, I will followe, blessed maist thou bee,
That thus releev'st thy foes in miserie. [*Exeunt.*

Lit.John   Skelton, a worde or two beside the play.

Frier   Now, Sir John Eltam, what ist you would say?

2210 **Lit.John** Me thinks I see no jeasts of Robin Hoode,
        No merry morices of Frier Tuck,
        No pleasant skippings up and downe the wodde,
        No hunting songs, no coursing of the bucke.
        Pray God this Play of ours may have good lucke,
2215   And the Kings Majestie mislike it not.

    Frier   And if he doe, what can we doe to that?
        I promist him a Play of Robin Hoode,
        His honorable life, in merry Sherewod;
        His Majestie himselfe survaid the plat,
2220   And bad me boldly write it, it was good,
        For merry jeasts, they have bene showne before,
        As how the Frier fell into the Well,
        For love of Jinny that faire bonny bell:
        How Greeneleafe robd the Shrieve of Notingham,
2225   And other mirthfull matter, full of game.
        Our play expresses noble Roberts wrong,
        His milde forgetting trecherous injurie;
        The Abbots malice, rak't in cinders long,
        Breakes out at last with Robins Tragedie.
2230   If these that heare the historie rehearst,
        Condemne my Play when it begins to spring,
        Ile let it wither while it is a budde,
        And never shewe the flower to the King.

    Lit.John One thing beside; you fall into your vaine,
2235   Of ribble rabble rimes, Skeltonicall,
        So oft, and stand so long, that you offend.

    Frier   It is a fault I hardly can amend.
        O how I champe my tongue to talke these tearmes,
        I doe forget oft times my Friers part;
2240   But pull mee by the sleeve when I exceede,
        And you shall see mee mend that fault indeede.
        Wherefore still sit you, doth Skelton intreat you,
        While he facetè wil breefely repeate you, the history al,
        And tale tragical, by whose treachery, and base injury,

2245   Robin the good, calde Robin Hood, died in Sherewodde:
        Which till, you see, be rul'd by me, sit patiently, and give
        a plaudite, if any thing please yee.   [*Exeunt. applause*

Scene xiv

[Enter Warman.

Warman   Banisht from all, of all I am bereft,
2250   No more than what I weare unto me left,
       O wretched, wretched griefe, desertfull fall.
       Striving to get all, I am reft of all;
       Yet if I could a while myselfe relieve,
       Till Ely be in some place settled,
2255   A double restitution should I get,
       And these sharpe sorrowes that have joy supprest
       Should turne to joy with double interest.

[Enter a gentleman, Warmans cosin.

       And in good time, here comes my cosin Warman,
2260   Whome I have often pleasur'd in my time.
       His house at Bingham I bestow'd on him;
       And therefore doubt not, he will give me house-roome.
       Good even, good cosin.

Cousin   O cousen Warman, what good newes with you?

2265   **Warman**   Whether so farre a foot walk you in Sherewod?

88

Cousin   I came from Rotheram, and by hither Farnsfield
My horse did tire, and I walkt home a foote.

Warman   I doe beseech you cousen at some friends,
Or at your owne house for a weeke or two,
2270   Give me some succour.

Cousin   Ha? Succour say you?
No, sir: I heard at Mansfield how the matter stands,
How you have justly lost your goods and lands,
And that the Princes indignation
2275   Will fall on any that relieves your state.
Away from mee; your trecheries I hate.
You when your noble master was undoone
(That honourable minded Huntington)
Who forwarder than you, all to distraine?
2280   And as a wolfe that chaseth on the plaine,
The harmelesse hinde, so wolfe-like you pursued
Him and his servants: vile ingratitude,
Damnd Judaisme, false wrong, abhorred trechery,
Impious wickednesse, wicked impietie.
2285   Out, out upon thee, foh, I spit at thee.

Warman   Good cosen.

Cousin   Away, Ile spurne thee if thou followe me. [*Exit.*

Warman   O just heaven, how thou plagu'st iniquitie!
All that he has, my hand on him bestowed.
2290   My master gave mee all I ever owed;
My master I abus'd in his distresse;
In mine, my kinsman leaves me comfortlesse.

[*Enter Jayler of Notingham, leading a dog.*

Here comes another, one that yesterday
2295   Was at my service, came when I did call,
And him I made Jayler of Notingham.
Perchance some pittie dwelles within the man.

89

Jaylor, well met, dost thou not knowe me, man?

Jailer   Yes, thou art Warman; every knave knowes thee.

2300   **Warman**   Thou knowest I was thy master yesterday.

Jailer   I, but tis not as it was, farewell, goe by.

Warman   Good George, relieve my bitter misery.

Jailer   By this fleshe and bloode I will not.
No if I do, the divell take me quicke.
2305   I have no money; begger balk the way.

Warman   I doe not aske thee money.

Jailer   Wouldst ha meate?

Warman   Would God I had a little breade to eate.

Jailer   Soft, let me feele my bagge. O heare is meate,
2310   That I put up at Redford for my dogge,
I care not greatly if I give him this.

Warman   I pre thee doe?

Jailer   Yet let me search my conscience for it first.
My dogge's my servant, faithfull, trustie, true;
2315   But Warman was a traitor to his Lord,
A reprobate, a rascall, and a Jewe,
Worser than dogges, of men to be abhorrd.
Starve therefore, Warman; dogge receive thy due;
Followe me not, least I belabour you,
2320   You halfe-fac't groat, you thin-cheekt chittiface,
You Judas, villane, you that have undoone
The honourable, Robert, Earle of Huntington. [*Exit.*

Warman   Worse than a dogge, the villane me respects,
His dogge he feedes, mee in my neede rejects.
2325   What shall I doe? Yonder I see a shed,

Scene xiv

A little cottage, where a woman dwelles,
Whose husband I from death delivered.
If she denie mee, then I faint and die.
Ho, goodwife Tomson?

2330 **Woman**   What a noyse is there?
A foule shame on yee; is it you that knockt?

Warman   What, doe you knowe mee then?

Woman   Whoop, who knowes not you?
The beggerd banisht Shrieve of Notingham,
2335 You that betraid your master, ist not you?
Yes, a shame on you; and forsooth ye come,
To have some succour here, because you sav'd,
My unthrift husband from the gallowe tree.
A pox upon yee both. Would both for me
2340 Were hangd together; but soft, let mee see.
The man lookes faint. Feelst thou indeede distresse?

Warman   O doe not mocke me in my heavinesse.

Woman   Indeede I doe not; well I have within,
A caudle made, I will goe fetch it him.

2345 **Warman**   O blessed woman, comfortable word.
Be quiet intrals, you shall be releev'd.

Woman   Here, Warman, put this hempen caudle ore thy head.
See downeward, yonder is thy masters walke,
And like a Judas, on some rotten tree,
2350 Hang up this rotten trunke of miserie
That goers by thy wretched end may see.
Stirr'st thou not villane? Get thee from my doore.
A plague upon thee, haste and hang thy selfe,
Runne rogue away. Tis thou that hast undone
2355 Thy noble master, Earle of Huntington. [*Exit.*

Warman   Good counsell, and good comfort by my faith.
Three doctors are of one opinion,

That Warman must make speede to hang himselfe.
The last hath given a caudle comfortable,
2360   That to recure my griefes is strong and able.
Ile take her medcine, and Ile chuse this way,
Wherein she saith my master hath his walke.
There will I offer life for trechery,
And hang, a wonder to all goers by.
2365   But soft what sound hermonious is this?
What birds are these, that sing so cheerefully,
As if they did salute the flowring spring?
Fitter it were, with tunes more dolefully
They shriekt out sorrowe than thus cheerely sing.
2370   I will goe seeke sad desperations cell.
This is not it, for here are greene-leav'd trees.
Ah for one winter-bitten bared bough,
Whereon, a wretched life, a wretch would leese.
O, here is one. Thrice blessed be this tree,
2375   If a man cursed, may a blessing give.

[*Enter old Fitzwater.*

But out alas, yonder comes one to me
To hinder death, when I detest to live.

Fitzwater What woefull voice heare I within this wod?
2380   What wretch is there complaines of wretchednesse?

Warman   A man, old man, bereav'd of all earths good,
And desperately seekes death in this distresse.

Fitzwater Seeke not for that which will be here too soone,
At least if thou be guiltie of ill deedes.
2385   Where art thou, sonne? Come and neerer sit;
Heare wholsome counsell gainst unhallowed thoughts.

Warman   The man is blinde. Muffle the eye of day
Ye gloomie clouds (and darker than my deedes,
That darker be than pitchie sable night),
2390   Muster together on these high topt trees,
That not a sparke of light thorough their sprayes,

Scene xiv

May hinder what I meane to execute.

Fitzwater What dost thou mutter? Heare mee wofull man.

[*Enter Marian, with meate.*

Marian God morrowe father.

Fitzwater Welcome, lovely maide,
And in good time, I trust you hither come.
Looke if you see not a distressefull man,
That to himselfe intendeth violence.
2400 One such even now was here and is not farre;
Seeke, I beseech you, save him if you may.

Marian Alas, here is, here is a man enrag'd,
Fastning a halter on a withered bough,
And stares upon mee, with such frighted lookes,
2405 As I am fearefull of his sharpe aspect.

Fitzwater What meanst thou, wretch? Say, what ist thou wilt doe?

Warman As Judas did, so I intend to doe.
For I have done alreadie as he did:
His master he betraid: so I have mine.
2410 Faire mistresse looke not on me with your blessed eyne.
From them as from some excellence divine,
Sparkles sharpe judgement, and commaunds with speede.
Faire, fare you well. Foule fortune is my fate.
As all betraiers, I die desperate.

2415 **Fitzwater** Soft sir, goe Marian call in Robin Hoode.
Tis Warman, woman, that was once his steward.

Marian Alas, although it be, yet save his life.
I will sende helpe unto you presently. [*Exit.*

Fitzwater Nay, Warman, stay; thou shalt not have thy will.

2420 **Warman** Art thou a blinde man, and canst see my shame?

To hinder treachers, God restoreth sight,
And giveth infants tongues to cry alowde,
A wofull woe against the trecherous.

[*Enter Much running.*

2425   **Much**   Hold, hold, hold. I heare say, my fellowe Warman
is about to hang himselfe, and make I some speede
to save him a labour. O good master, Justice Shrive,
have you execution in hand, and is there such a murren
among theeves and hangmen, that you play two parts
2430   in one? For old inquaintance, I wil play one part. The knot
under the eare, the knitting to the tree: Good master
Warman, leave that worke for mee.

    Warman   Dispatch me, Much, and I will pray for thee.

    Much   Nay, keepe your praiers; no bodie sees us.

2435   [*He takes the rope, and offers to clime.*

    Fitzwater   Downe sirra, downe; whether a knaves name
clime you?

    Much   A plague on ye for a blinde sinksanker. Would I *sooth-*
sayer
    were your match. You are much blinde yfaith, can hit
2440   so right.

    [*Enter Little John.*

    Lit.John   What, master Warman, are yee come to yield
A true account for your false stewardshippe?

    [*Enter Scarlet and Scathlocke.*

2445   **Scathlock**   Much, if thou meanst to get a hundred pound,
Present us to the Shrieve of Notingham.

    Much   Masse, I thinke there was such a purclamation.

Come, my small fellowe John,
You shall have halfe, and therefore bring in one.

2450 **Lit.John**   No, my big fellow, honest master Much,
Take all unto yourselfe; Ile be no halfe.

Much   Then stand, you shall be the two theeves, and
I will be the presenter.
O master Shrieve of Notingham,
2455 When eares unto my tidings came
(Ile speake in prose, I misse this verse vilely) that   *mismeter*
Scathlock and Scarlet were arrested by Robin Hood, my
master, and Little John, my fellowe, and I, Much his servant, and taken from you, master Shrieve, being well
2460 forward in the hanging way, wherein yee now are (and
God keepe yee in the same) and also that you, master Shrieve,
would give any man in towne, citie, or contrey, a hundred pound of lawfull arrant money of Englande, that
would bring the same two theeves, being these two. Now
2465 I, the said Much, chalenge of you, the saide Shrieve,
bringing them, the same money.

Scarlet   Faith, he can not pay thee, Much.

Much   I, but while this end is in my hand, and that about
his necke, he is bound to it.

2470   [*Enter Robin, Ely, Marian.*

Warman   Mock on, mock on; make me your jeasting game.
I doe deserve much more than this small shame.

Robin   Disconsolate and poore dejected man,
Cast from thy necke that shamefull signe of death,
2475 And live for mee, if thou amende thy life,
As much in favour as thou ever didst.

Warman   O worse than any death,
When a man, wrongd, his wronger pittieth.

Ely   Warman, be comforted, rise and amend.
2480   On my word, Robin Hoode will be thy friend.

Robin   I will indeede. Go in, heart-broken man,
Father Fitzwater, pray you leade him in.
Kinde Marian, with sweete comforts comfort him,
And my tall yeomen, as you mee affect,
2485   Upbraide him not with his forepassed life.
Warman, goe in, goe in and comfort thee.

Warman   O God requite your honours curtesie.

Marian   Scathlocke or Scarlet, helpe us some of yee.

    [*Exeunt Warman, Marian, Fitzwater, Scathlock, Scarlet, Much*
2490   *Enter Frier Tucke in his trusse, without his weede.*]

Frier   Jesu benedicité, pittie on pittie, mercie on mercy,
misery on misery. O such a sight, as by this light, doth
mee affright.

Robin   Tell us the matter, pre thee, holy Frier.

2495 **Frier**   Sir Doncaster the Priest, and the proud Prior
Are stript and wounded in the way to Bawtrey,
And if there goe not spedie remedie,
Theyl die, theyl die in this extreamitie.

Robin   Alas, direct us to that wretched place.
2500   I love mine uncle, though he hateth mee.

Frier   My weede I cast to keepe them from the colde,
And Jinny, gentle girle, tore all her smocke,
The blodie issue of their wounds to stoppe.

Robin   Will you goe with us, my good Lord of Ely?

2505 **Ely**   I will, and ever praise thy perfect charitie.
                [*Exeunt.*

Scene xv

[*Enter Prince John, solus, in greene, bowe and arrowes.*   *alone*

Pr. John   Why this is somewhat like, now may I sing,
As did the Wakefield Pinder in his note;
At Michaelmas commeth my covenant out,
2510   My master gives me my fee.
Then, Robin, Ile weare thy Kendall greene,
And wend to the greenewodde with thee.
But for a name now, John, it must not bee,
Alreadie Little John on him attends.
2515   Greeneleafe? Nay surely there's such a one alreadie.
Well, Ile be Wodnet, hap what happen may.

    [*Enter Scathlocke.*

Here comes a greene cote (good lucke be my guide).
Some sodaine shift might helpe me to provide.

2520 **Scathlock**   What, fellow William, did you meete our master?

Pr. John   I did not meete him yet my honest friend.

Scathlock   My honest friend? Why, what a terme is here?
My name is Scathlocke, man, and if thou be
No other than thy garments shewe to mee,

97

2525   Thou art my fellowe, though I knowe thee not.
        What is thy name? When wert thou entertaind?

Pr. John   My name is Woodnet, and this very day,
        My noble master, Earle of Huntington,
        Did give mee both my fee and liverie.

2530 **Scathlock** Your noble master, Earle of Huntington?
        Ile lay a crowne you are a counterfait,
        And that you knowe, lacks money of a noble.
        Did you receive your livery and fee,
        And never heared our orders read unto you?
2535   What was the oath was given you by the Frier?

Pr. John   Who? Frier Tuck? [*Enter Frier Tucke.*

Scathlock I doe not play the lyer;
        For he comes here himselfe to shrive.

Pr. John   Scathlock, farewell, I will away.

2540 **Scathlock** See you this arrowe? It saies nay.
        Through both your sides shall fly this feather,
        If presently you come not hither.

Frier   Now heavens true liberalitie
        Fall ever for his charitie
2545   Upon the heade of Robin Hoode,
        That to his very foes doth good.
        Lord God, how he laments the Prior
        And bathes his wounds against the fier!
        Faire Marian, God requite it her,
2550   Doth even as much for Doncaster,
        Whome newly she hath laine in bed,
        To rest his weary wounded head.

Scathlock Ho, Frier Tuck, knowe you this mate?

Frier   Whats hee?

2555 **Scathlock** He saith my master late
Gave him his fee and livery.

Frier   It is a leasing, credit mee.
How chance, sir, then you were not sworne?

Pr. John What meane this groome and lozell Frier,
2560   So strictly matters to inquire?
Had I a sword and buckler here,
You should aby these questions deare.

Frier   Saist thou me so lad? Lend him thine.
For in this bush here lyeth mine.
2565   Now will I try this newcome guest.

Scathlock I am his first man, Frier Tuck,
And if I faile and have no lucke,
Then thou with him shalt have a plucke.

Frier   Be it so Scathlock. Holde thee lad,
2570   No better weapons can be had.
The dewe doth them a little rust.
But heare yee, they are tooles of trust.

Pr. John Gramercy Frier for this gift,
And if thou come unto my shrift,
2575   Ile make thee call those fellowes fooles
That on their foes bestowe such tooles.

Scathlock Come let us too't.

[*Fight, and the Frier lookes on.*

Frier   The youth is deliver and light,
He presseth Scathlocke with his might:
Now by my beades to doe him right,
I thinke he be some tryed knight.

Scathlock Stay, let us breath.

Pr. John   I will not stay.
2585   If you leave, Frier, come away.

Scathlock I pre the, Frier, holde him play.

Frier   Frier Tuck will doe the best he may.

[*Fight. Enter Marian.*

Marian   Why, what a noyse of swordes is here?
2590   Fellowes, and fight our bower so neere?

Scathlock Mistresse, he is no man of yours,
        That fightes so fast with Frier Tucke;
        But on my worde he is a man,
        As good for strength as any can.

2595   **Marian**   Indeede hee's more than common men can be,
        In his high heart there dwels the bloode of kings.
        Goe call my Robin, Scathlock: tis Prince John.

Scathlock Mistresse I will; I pray part the fray.   [*Exit.*

Marian   I pre thee goe; I will doe what I may.
2600   Frier, I charge thee holde thy hand.

Frier   Nay, yonker, to your tackling stand.
        What all amort, wil you not fight?

Pr. John   I yield, unconquered by thy might,
        But by Matildas glorious sight.

2605   **Frier**   Mistresse, he knowes you. What is hee?

Pr. John Like to amazing wonder she appeares,
        And from her eye, flies love unto my heart,
        Attended by suspicious thoughts and feares,
        That numme the vigor of each outward part.
2610   Only my sight hath all sacietie,
        And fulnesse of delight, viewing her deitie.

Marian But I have no delight in you, Prince John.

Frier Is this Prince John?
Give me thy hand, thou art a proper man,
2615 And for this mornings worke, by Saints above,
Be ever sure of Frier Tucks true love.

Pr. John Be not offended that I touch thy shrine;
Make this hand happie, let it folde in thine.

[*Enter Robin Hoode, Fitzwater, Ely, Warman.*

2620 **Robin** What sawcie wodman Marian stands so neere?

Pr. John A wodman, Robin, that would strike your deere,
With all his heart. Nay never looke so strange,
You see this fickle world is full of change.
John is a ranger, man, compeld to range.

2625 **Fitzwater** You are young, wilde Lord, and wel may travel bear.

Pr. John What, my olde friende Fitzwater, are you there?
And you, Lord Ely? And old best betrust?
Then I perceive that to this geere we must.
A messe of my good friends, which of you foure
2630 Will purchase thanks by yielding to the King
The bodie of the rash rebellious John?
Will you, Fitzwater?

Fitzwater No, John, I defie
To stain my old hands in thy youthfull bloode.

2635 **Pr. John** You will, Lord Ely, I am sure you will.

Ely Be sure, young man, my age means thee no ill.

Pr. John O you will have the praise, brave Robin Hood,
The lustie outlawe, Lord of this large wodde.
Hee'l lead a kings sonne, prisoner to a king,

2640   And bid the brother smite the brother deade.

    Robin My purpose you have much misconstrued.
    Prince John, I would not for the wide worlds wealth
    Incense his Majestie, but doe my best,
    To mitigate his wrath, if he be mov'd.

2645 **Pr. John** Will none of you? Then here's one I dare say,
    That from his childehoode knowes how to betray.
    Warman, will not you helpe to hinder all you may.

    Warman With what I have beene, twit me not, my Lord.
    My olde sins at my soule I doe detest.

2650 **Pr. John** Then that he came this way, Prince John was blest.
    Forgive me, Ely; pardon mee, Fitzwater.
    And Robin, to thy hands myselfe I yield.

    Robin And as my heart, from hurt I will thee shield.

    [*Enter Much, running.*

2655 **Much** Master, fly, hide ye mistresse, we al shall be taken.

    Robin Why, whats the matter?

    Much The King, the King, and twelve and twenty score of
horses.

    Robin Peace, foole. We have no cause from him to fly.

    [*Enter Scarlet, Little John.*

2660 **Lit.John** Scarlet and I were hunting on the plaine.
    To us came royall Richard from his traine
    (For a great traine of his is hard at hand)
    And questiond us, if we serv'd Robin Hoode.
    I saide wee did, and then his Majestie,
2665   Putting this massie chaine about my necke,
    Said what I shame to say, but joyde to heare.

Let Scarlet tell it, it befits not mee.

Scarlet   Quoth our good King, "Thy name is Little John,
And thou hast long time serv'd Earle Huntington:
2670   Because thou leftst him not in miserie,
A hundred markes I give thee yearelie fee,
And from henceforth, thou shalt a squier bee."

Much   O Lord, what luck had I to runne away?
I should have bene made a knight, or a lady sure.

2675   **Scarlet**   Goe, said the King, and to your master say,
Richard is come to call him to the court.
And with his kingly presence chase the clouds
Of griefe and sorrow, that in mistie shades,
Have vaild the honour of Earle Huntington.

2680   **Robin**   Now God preserve him, hye you backe againe,
And guide him, least in by-paths he mistake.   *lest;*
Much, fetch a richer garment for my father.
              [*Exit Much.*
Good Frier Tuck, I pre thee rouse thy wits.
Warman, visit myne uncle and Sir Doncaster,
2685   See if they can come forth to grace our showe.
              [*Exit Warman.*
Gods pittie, Marian, let your Jinny waite.
Thankes, my Lord Chancellor. You are well prepar'd,
And good Prince John, since you are all in greene,
Disdaine not to attend on Robin Hoode.
2690   Frolick I pray; I trust to doe yee good.
Welcome, good uncle, welcome Sir Doncaster.
              [*Enter Prior and Doncast.*
Say, will yee sit, I feare yee cannot stand.

Prior   Yes, very well.

Robin   Why, cheerely, cheerely then.
2695   The trumpet, sounds, the King is now at hand.
Lords, yeomen, maids, in decent order stand.

[The trumpets sound, the while Robin places them.
Enter first, bare-heade, Little John and Scarlet; likewise
Chester, and Lester, bearing the sword and scepter; the
2700   *King follows crowned, clad in green; after him Queene*
Mother, after her Salsbury and Richmond, Scarlet and
Scathlocke turne to Robin Hoode; who with all his
company kneele downe and cry:

All   God save King Richard, Lord preserve your Grace.

2705   **King**   Thanks all, but chiefely, Huntington, to thee.
            Arise poore Earle, stand up, my late lost sonne,
            And on thy shoulders let me rest my armes,
            That have bene toyled long with heathen warres:
            True piller of my state, right Lord indeede,
2710   Whose honour shineth in the denne of neede,
            I am even full of joy, and full of woe;
            To see thee, glad; but sad to see thee so.

    Robin   O that I could powre out my soule in prayers,
            And praises for this kingly curtesie.
2715   Doe not, dread Lord, grieve at my lowe estate.
            Never so rich, never so fortunate,
            Was Huntington as now himselfe he findes.
            And to approve it, may it please your Grace,
            But to accept such presents at the hand
2720   Of your poore servant, as he hath prepar'd.
            You shall perceive, the Emperour of the East,
            Whom you contended with at Babilon,
            Had not such presents to present you with.

    King   Art thou so rich? Sweet, let me see thy gifts.

2725   **Robin**   First take againe this jewell you had lost,
            Aged Fitzwater, banished by John.

    King   A jemme indeede; no Prince hath such a one.
            Good, good old man, as welcome unto mee,
            As coole fresh ayre, in heats extreamitie.

2730 **Fitzwater** And I as glad to kisse my soveraignes hand,
As the wrackt swimmer, when he feeles the land.

Queene   Welcome, Fitzwater, I am glad to see you.

Fitzwater I thanke your Grace; but let me hug these twain,
Lester and Richmond, Christes sworne champions,
2735 That follow'd Richard in his holy warre.

Richmond Noble Fitzwater, thanks, and welcome both.

Leicester O God, how glad I am to see this Lord!
I cannot speake; but welcome at a worde.

Robin   Next take good Ely in your royall hands,
2740 Who fled from death, and most uncivill bands.

King   Robin, thy gifts exceede: Moorton my Chancellour!
In this man giv'st thou holinesse and honour.

Ely   Indeede he gives me, and he gave me life,
Preserving me from fierce pursuing foes,
2745 When I too blame had wrought him many woes:
With me he likewise did preserve this seale,
Which I surrender to your majestie.

King   Keepe it, good Ely, keepe it still for me.

Robin   The next faire jewell that I will presente
2750 Is richer than both these, yet in the foyle,
My gratious Lord, it hath a foule default,
Which if you pardon, boldly I protest,
It will in value farre exceede the rest.

Pr. John [*Aside*] Thats me he meanes, yfaith my turne is next.
2755 He calles me foile, ifaith, I feare a foile.
Well, tis a mad lord, this same Huntington.

Robin   Here is Prince John, your brother, whose revolt
And folly in your absence, let me crave,

2760

With his submission may be buried.
For he is now no more the man he was,
But duetifull in all respects to you.

King   Pray God it proove so. Wel, good Huntington,
For thy sake pardon'd is our brother John,
And welcome to us in all heartie love.

2765 **Robin**   This last I give, as tenants do their lands,
With a surrender, to receive againe,
The same into their owne possession:
No Marian, but Fitzwaters chast Matilda,
The precious jewell that poore Huntington
2770   Doth in this world hold as his best esteeme.
Although with one hand I surrender her,
I holde the other, as one looking still,
Richard returnes her: so I hope he will.

King   Els God forbid. Receive thy Marian backe,
2775   And never may your love be separate,
But florish fairely to the utmost date.

Robin   Now please my King to enter Robins bower,
And take such homely welcome as he findes,
It shall be reckened as my happinesse.

2780 **King**   With all my heart. Then as combined friends,
Goe we togither; here all quarrelles ends. [*Exeunt.*

[*Manet Sir John Eltam and Skelton.*

Eltham   Then Skelton here I see you will conclude.

Skelton   And reason good: have we not held too long?

2785 **Eltham**   No in good sadnesse, I dare gage my life,
His Highnesse will accept it very kindly.
But I assure you, he expects withall,
To see the other matters tragicall
That followe in the processe of the storie,

2790 Wherein are many a sad accident,
   Able to make the strictest minde relent:
   I neede not name the points, you knowe them all.
   From Marians eye shall not one teare be shed?
   Skelton, yfaith tis not the fashion.
2795 The King must greeve, the Queene must take it ill;
   Ely must mourne, aged Fitzwater weepe,
   Prince John, the Lords his yeomen must lament,
   And wring their wofull hands, for Robins woe.
   Then must the sicke man fainting by degrees,
2800 Speake hollowe words, and yield his Marian,
   Chast Maid Matilda, to her fathers hands
   And give her, with King Richards full consent,
   His lands, his goods, late seazd on by the Prior,
   Now by the Priors treason made the Kings.
2805 Skelton, there are a many other things,
   That aske long time to tell them lineally.
   But ten times longer will the action be.

Skelton Sir John, yfaith I knowe not what to doe;
   And I confesse that all you say is true.
2810 Will you doe one thing for me, crave the King
   To see two parts. Say tis a prettie thing.
   I know you can doe much, if you excuse mee,
   While Skelton lives, Sir John, be bolde to use mee.

Eltham I will perswade the King; but how can you
2815 Perswade all these beholders to content?

Skelton Stay, Sir John Eltam; what to them I say,
   Deliver to the King, from mee, I pray.
   Well judging hearers, for a while suspence
   Your censures of this Plaies unfinisht end.
2820 And Skelton promises for this offence,
   The second part shall presently be pend.
   There shall you see, as late my friend did note,
   King Richards revels at Earle Roberts bower,
   The purpos'd mirth, and the performed mone,
2825 The death of Robin, and his murderers.
   For interest of your stay, this will I adde,

King Richards voyage backe to Austria,
The swift returned tydings of his death,
The manner of his royall funerall.
2830   Then John shall be a lawfull crowned king,
But to Matilda beare unlawfull love.
Aged Fitzwaters finall banishment,
His pitious end, of power teares to move
From marble pillers. The Catastrophe
2835   Shall shewe you faire Matildas Tragedie,
Who, shunning Johns pursute, became a nunne,
At Dunmowe Abbey, where she constantly
Chose death to save her spotlesse chastitie.
Take but my word, and if I faile in this,
2840   Then let my paines be baffled with a hisse.

FINIS.

Also from Benediction Books ...

Wandering Between Two Worlds: Essays on Faith and Art
Anita Mathias
Benediction Books, 2007
152 pages
ISBN: 0955373700

Available from www.amazon.com, www.amazon.co.uk
www.wanderingbetweentwoworlds.com

In these wide-ranging lyrical essays, Anita Mathias writes, in lush, lovely prose, of her naughty Catholic childhood in Jamshedpur, India; her large, eccentric family in Mangalore, a sea-coast town converted by the Portuguese in the sixteenth century; her rebellion and atheism as a teenager in her Himalayan boarding school, run by German missionary nuns, St. Mary's Convent, Nainital; and her abrupt religious conversion after which she entered Mother Teresa's convent in Calcutta as a novice. Later rich, elegant essays explore the dualities of her life as a writer, mother, and Christian in the United States-- Domesticity and Art, Writing and Prayer, and the experience of being "an alien and stranger" as an immigrant in America, sensing the need for roots.

About the Author

Anita Mathias was born in India, has a B.A. and M.A. in English from Somerville College, Oxford University and an M.A. in Creative Writing from the Ohio State University. Her essays have been published in The Washington Post, The London Magazine, The Virginia Quarterly Review, Commonweal, Notre Dame Magazine, America, The Christian Century, Religion Online, The Southwest Review, Contemporary Literary Criticism, New Letters, The Journal, and two of HarperSanFrancisco's The Best Spiritual Writing anthologies. Her non-fiction has won fellowships from The National Endowment for the Arts; The Minnesota State Arts Board; The Jerome Foundation, The Vermont Studio Center; The Virginia Centre for the Creative Arts, and the First Prize for the Best General Interest Article from the Catholic Press Association of the United States and Canada. Anita has taught Creative Writing at the College of William and Mary, and now lives and writes in Oxford, England.

"Yesterday's Treasures for Today's Readers"
Titles by Benediction Classics available from Amazon.co.uk

Religio Medici, Hydriotaphia, Letter to a Friend, Thomas Browne

Pseudodoxia Epidemica: Or, Enquiries into Commonly Presumed Truths, Thomas Browne

Urne Buriall and The Garden of Cyrus, Thomas Browne

The Maid's Tragedy, Beaumont and Fletcher

The Custom of the Country, Beaumont and Fletcher

Philaster Or Love Lies a Bleeding, Beaumont and Fletcher

A Treatise of Fishing with an Angle, Dame Juliana Berners.

Pamphilia to Amphilanthus, Lady Mary Wroth

The Compleat Angler, Izaak Walton

The Magnetic Lady, Ben Jonson

Every Man Out of His Humour, Ben Jonson

The Masque of Blacknesse. The Masque of Beauty,. Ben Jonson

The Life of St. Thomas More, William Roper

Pendennis, William Makepeace Thackeray

Salmacis and Hermaphroditus attributed to Francis Beaumont

Friar Bacon and Friar Bungay Robert Greene

Holy Wisdom, Augustine Baker

The Jew of Malta and the Massacre at Paris, Christopher Marlowe

Tamburlaine the Great, Parts 1 & 2 AND Massacre at Paris, Christopher Marlowe

All Ovids Elegies, Lucans First Booke, Dido Queene of Carthage, Hero and Leander, Christopher Marlowe

The Titan, Theodore Dreiser

Scapegoats of the Empire: The true story of the Bushveldt Carbineers, George Witton

All Hallows' Eve, Charles Williams

The Place of The Lion, Charles Williams

The Greater Trumps, Charles Williams

My Apprenticeship: Volumes I and II, Beatrice Webb

Last and First Men / Star Maker, Olaf Stapledon

Last and First Men, Olaf Stapledon

Darkness and the Light, Olaf Stapledon

The Worst Journey in the World, Apsley Cherry-Garrard

The Schoole of Abuse, Containing a Pleasaunt Invective Against Poets, Pipers, Plaiers, Iesters and Such Like Catepillers of the Commonwelth, Stephen Gosson

Russia in the Shadows, H. G. Wells

Wild Swans at Coole, W. B. Yeats

A hundreth good pointes of husbandrie, Thomas Tusser

The Collected Works of Nathanael West: "The Day of the Locust", "The Dream Life of Balso Snell", "Miss Lonelyhearts", "A Cool Million", Nathanael West

Miss Lonelyhearts & The Day of the Locust, Nathaniel West

The Worst Journey in the World, Apsley Cherry-Garrard

Scott's Last Expedition, V1, R. F. Scott

The Dream of Gerontius, John Henry Newman

The Brother of Daphne, Dornford Yates

The Downfall of Robert Earl of Huntington, Anthony Munday

Clayhanger, Arnold Bennett

The Regent, A Five Towns Story Of Adventure In London , Arnold Bennett

The Card, A Story Of Adventure In The Five Towns , Arnold Bennett

South: The Story of Shackleton's Last Expedition 1914-1917, Sir Ernest Shackketon

Greene's Groatsworth of Wit: Bought With a Million of Repentance, Robert Greene

Beau Sabreur, Percival Christopher Wren

The Hekatompathia, or Passionate Centurie of Love, Thomas Watson

The Art of Rhetoric, Thomas Wilson

Stepping Heavenward, Elizabeth Prentiss

Barker's Delight, or The Art of Angling, Thomas Barker

The Napoleon of Notting Hill, G.K. Chesterton

The Douay-Rheims Bible (The Challoner Revision)

Endimion - The Man in the Moone, John Lyly

Gallathea and Midas, John Lyly,

Mother Bombie, John Lyly

Manners, Custom and Dress During the Middle Ages and During the Renaissance Period, Paul Lacroix

Obedience of a Christian Man, William Tyndale

St. Patrick for Ireland, James Shirley

The Wrongs of Woman; Or Maria/Memoirs of the Author of a Vindication of the Rights of Woman, Mary Wollstonecraft and William Godwin

De Adhaerendo Deo. Of Cleaving to God, Albertus Magnus

Obedience of a Christian Man, William Tyndale

A Trick to Catch the Old One, Thomas Middleton

The Phoenix, Thomas Middleton

A Yorkshire Tragedy, Thomas Middleton (attrib.)

The Princely Pleasures at Kenelworth Castle, George Gascoigne

The Fair Maid of the West. Part I and Part II. Thomas Heywood

Proserpina, Volume I and Volume II. Studies of Wayside Flowers, John Ruskin

Our Fathers Have Told Us. Part I. The Bible of Amiens. John Ruskin

The Poetry of Architecture: Or the Architecture of the Nations of Europe Considered in Its Association with Natural Scenery and National Character, John Ruskin

The Endeavour Journal of Sir Joseph Banks. Sir Joseph Banks

Christ Legends: And Other Stories, Selma Lagerlof; (trans. Velma Swanston Howard)

Chamber Music, James Joyce

Blurt, Master Constable, Thomas Middleton, Thomas Dekker

Since Yesterday, Frederick Lewis Allen

The Scholemaster: Or, Plaine and Perfite Way of Teachyng Children the Latin Tong , Roger Ascham

The Wonderful Year, 1603, Thomas Dekker

Waverley, Sir Walter Scott

Guy Mannering, Sir Walter Scott

Old Mortality, Sir Walter Scott

The Knight of Malta, John Fletcher

The Double Marriage, John Fletcher and Philip Massinger

Space Prison, Tom Godwin

The Home of the Blizzard Being the Story of the Australasian Antarctic Expedition, 1911-1914, Douglas Mawson

Wild-goose Chase , John Fletcher

If You Know Not Me, You Know Nobody. Part I and Part II, Thomas Heywood

The Ragged Trousered Philanthropists, Robert Tressell

The Island of Sheep, John Buchan

Eyes of the Woods, Joseph Altsheler

The Club of Queer Trades, G. K. Chesterton

The Financier, Theodore Dreiser

Something of Myself, Rudyard Kipling

Law of Freedom in a Platform, or True Magistracy Restored, Gerrard Winstanley

Damon and Pithias, Richard Edwards

Dido Queen of Carthage: And, The Massacre at Paris, Christopher Marlowe

Cocoa and Chocolate: Their History from Plantation to Consumer, Arthur Knapp

Lady of Pleasure, James Shirley

The South Pole: An account of the Norwegian Antarctic expedition in the "Fram," 1910-12. Volume 1 and Volume 2, Roald Amundsen

A Yorkshire Tragedy, Thomas Middleton (attrib.)

The Tragedy of Soliman and Perseda, Thomas Kyd

The Rape of Lucrece. Thomas Heywood

Myths and Legends of Ancient Greece and Rome, E. M. Berens

In the Forbidden Land, Henry Savage Arnold Landor

Across Unknown South America, by Arnold Henry Savage Landor

Illustrated History of Furniture: From the Earliest to the Present Time, Frederick Litchfield

A Narrative of Some of the Lord's Dealings with George Müller Written by Himself (Parts I-IV, 1805-1856), George Müller

The Towneley Cycle Of The Mystery Plays (Or The Wakefield Cycle): Thirty-Two Pageants, Anonymous

The Insatiate Countesse, John Marston.

Spontaneous Activity in Education, Maria Montessori.

On the Art of Writing, Sir Arthur Quiller-Couch

The Well of the Saints, J. M. Synge

Bacon's Advancement Of Learning And The New Atlantis, Francis Bacon.

Catholic Tales And Christian Songs, Dorothy Sayers.

Two Little Savages: Being the Adventures of Two Boys who Lived as Indians and What they Learned, Ernest Thompson Seton

The Sadness of Christ, Thomas More

The Family of Love, Thomas Middleton

The Passing of the Aborigines: A Lifetime Spent Among the Natives of Australia, Daisy Bates

The Children, Edith Wharton

A Record of European Armour and Arms through Seven Centuries., (Volumes I, II, III, IV and V) Francis Laking

The Book of the Farm: - Detailing The Labours Of The Farmer, Steward, Plowman, Hedger, Cattle-Man, Shepherd, Field-Worker, and Dairymaid. (Volume I), Henry Stephens

The Book of the Farm: - Detailing The Labours Of The Farmer, Steward, Plowman, Hedger, Cattle-Man, Shepherd, Field-Worker, and Dairymaid. (Volume II), Henry Stephens

The Book of the Farm: - Detailing The Labours Of The Farmer, Steward, Plowman, Hedger, Cattle-Man, Shepherd, Field-Worker, and Dairymaid. (Volume III). by Henry Stephens

The Naturalist On The River Amazons, by Henry Walter Bates.

Antarctic Penguins: A Study of their Social Habits, Dr. George Murray Levick

and many others…

www.ingramcontent.com/pod-product-compliance
Lightning Source LLC
Chambersburg PA
CBHW021200020426
42331CB00003B/141